CONTENTS

Ships in Focus Publications

Correspondence and editorial:
Roy Fenton
18 Durrington Avenue
London SW20 8NT
020 8879 3527
record@rfenton.co.uk

Orders and photographic:
John & Marion Clarkson
18 Franklands, Longton
Preston PR4 5PD
01772 612855
shipsinfocus@btinternet.com

Printed by Amadeus Press Ltd.,
Cleckheaton, Yorkshire.
Designed by Hugh Smallwood, John Clarkson and Roy Fenton.

SHIPS IN FOCUS RECORD
ISBN 978-1-901703-27-6

SUBSCRIPTION RATES FOR RECORD

Readers can start their subscription with any issue, and are welcome to backdate it to receive previous issues.

	3 issues	4 issues
UK	£24	£31
Europe (airmail)	£26	£34
Rest of the world (surface mail)	£26	£34
Rest of the world (airmail)	£31	£41

SHIPS IN FOC[US]
Noven[mber]

As the reader would expect, a large num[ber...] preparation of 'Record', especially when compiling [...] essentially pictorial, like the South West Scenes series. There are so many publications referred to that, even if the editor responsible could remember every one he used, listing them in each issue would be tedious. Hence a blanket acknowledgement must suffice, especially to all those authors who have toiled away to include fleet lists in their books.

Any such book will contain a huge amount of data, and to access it an index of ship names is absolutely vital, and not just those names carried whilst in the fleet under consideration. Yet too many authors or publishers neglect one, or sell the reader short. Sure, indexing ships is hard work, but how else can a mass of painstakingly-collected data be made readily available? Indexing can only be done at the last minute, when page proofs are available, and often when the printer is howling for the final copy. In many of its otherwise excellent paperback fleet lists, the World Ship Society took a short cut and simply indexed the ship according to the number of the fleet list entry, rather than the page, and omitted any references to or photographs of ships in the company history section. This might have worked when there was just one fleet list, but in certain books – for example, those on Salvesen and Strick – the user had to search through a multitude of lists to find a particular ship. No, the only safe method is to index every ship by page number, and let the printer wait.

In customary fashion, and practising what we preach, this issue - the fourth of our notional fourteenth volume - contains the index to issues 53 to 56 compiled by Heather Fenton, and to accommodate it we have included eight extra pages.

Some years ago we offered a cumulative index up to and including issue 28. Uptake was not as great as we had hoped, but the exercise was very helpful to the compilers. We are now in the throes of repeating the process, and producing a cumulative index of all articles and ships mentioned or illustrated up to and including the present issue, number 56. Later this year it will available on a CD for a nominal £2.50 (to cover the cost of the disk and postage, and help toward's Mrs Fenton's pocket money). Please contact our London address to order a copy.

Even after 56 'Records', the editors find it difficult to predict just how many articles to prepare for each issue, as this very largely depends on how many photographs are found. For this issue we reached 72 pages before two of the planned fearures were completely edited, and so 'Fleet in Focus' and 'Putting the Record straight' have been held over until issue 57.

Lastly, an apology. In the contents page of 'Record' 55 an out-of-date e-mail address was quoted for Roy Fenton: he can be contacted on record@rfenton.co.uk

John Clarkson   Roy Fenton

Saint Tudwal appears to be staggering into Preston Dock. From 1925 to 1929 her owners were associated with the Great Yarmouth Shipping Co. Ltd., whose history starts overleaf. *[World Ship Society Ltd.]*

Henry Newhouse was a predecessor of the Great Yarmouth company. The 17-year-old *Eastern Counties* (right) was acquired by him in 1907 but capsized and sank near Spurn Point in October 1911. She was replaced by the 1898-built *Ape* (middle) in 1912, but on her sale in 1916 Newhouse was left without ships. *[Barnard and Straker/J. and M. Clarkson].*

Seen towing a lighter (bottom), the steam wherry *Opal* was built at Gainsborough in 1896 for John Crisp and Son, Beccles, who were acquired by General Steam in 1906. She was among the group of river craft sold for scrap in 1960 after coal deliveries to Norwich Gas Works ceased. *[John Baker collection]*

GREAT YARMOUTH SHIPPING CO. LTD.
Part 1
Roy Fenton

This company is an example of the local shipping lines that were important to their communities, but which were to become small cogs in much larger, national organisations. Almost inevitably, they have long since succumbed to competition and to changing trading patterns, which mean that small ports such as Yarmouth no longer handle general merchandise.

Origins

The precursors of the Great Yarmouth Shipping Co. Ltd. were several small and relatively short-lived shipping lines (see diagram overleaf).

During the 1890s, a Henry Newhouse began to operate a thrice-weekly shipping service between Yarmouth and Hull. The late Mike Stammers (see 'Sources and Acknowledgements') gave 1892 as the date for the opening of this service, although Newhouse's first ship was the 341gt *Amelia*, delivered new to him by S. McKnight and Co. of Ayr in September 1894. Newhouse's small fleet had a rapid turnover, with *Amelia* being replaced in 1900 by *Flamingo* (255/1885) and *Norfolk* (299/1887), with the latter giving way just two years later to the new *Yarmouth* (438/1902). In 1907 she was in turn replaced by *Eastern Counties* (458/1890). His last ship was the former Burns steamer *Ape* (439/1898), bought in 1912 and sold in 1916 after Newhouse's services had been curtailed by the First World War. Under the title Yare and Waveney Lighter Co. Ltd., Newhouse also had lighters, tugs and other small craft employed between Yarmouth and Norwich, including the steel-hulled *Opal* of 1896, described as a 'steam wherry'. He also operated warehousing and distribution services for merchandise, including ABC Wharves at both Yarmouth and Norwich. Stammers gave the title ABC Shipping Co. Ltd. to his shipping company, but no ships have been found which were registered in this name.

In 1919 the trade between Hull and Yarmouth was re-opened under the title Hull and Yarmouth Steamship Service. It is possible that Newhouse was still involved, as some of his wharves continued to be used, although the operator of the revived Hull service was Cartwright, Wenn and Co. Ltd. Of its principals, Arthur Cartwright was associated with T. Small and Co. Ltd., the Yarmouth shipbrokers, whilst Frederick Wenn was a timber merchant and sawmill operator. Under the title Wenn Ltd. the latter had the iron steamer *Sagittarius* (195/1887) which inaugurated the post-war Hull service. Wenn's withdrawal in 1921 precipitated a merger of the Cartwright, Wenn company with T. Small and Co. Ltd., the resultant concern becoming T. Small and Co. (Great Yarmouth) Ltd. Also involved was a Frederick Spashett of Lowestoft, who became Chairman and who also bought the aging iron steamer *Clansman* (302/1880), presumably to replace *Sagittarius*.

The General Steam Navigation Co. Ltd. was also interested in Yarmouth as they operated services between Norwich, Lowestoft and London as a result of their 1906 acquisition of John Crisp and Son, Beccles. In 1923 an amalgamation of local shipping services was agreed, and on 15th June the Great Yarmouth Shipping Co. Ltd. was registered at 18 Regent Road, Great Yarmouth. The Hull service was taken over from T. Small and Co. (Great Yarmouth) Ltd., in consideration of which the latter concern was given shares in the Great Yarmouth Shipping Co. Ltd. valued at £4,000. General Steam was the largest initial shareholder in the new company, other investors including I.M. Hooper of London and Frederick Spashett, who continued on the board, although not as Chairman, until his death in 1945. Secretary and manager for registration purposes was Henry I. Colville, who in 1925 was to register a steamer in his own right, the *Saint Tudwal*. Colville was also to enjoy a long association with the company, continuing as Secretary until his death in 1953.

Spashett's *Clansman* was quickly transferred to the new company, although she foundered on the service to Hull during October 1924, the Great Yarmouth company's only peacetime loss. The *Ivytown* and *City of Malines* followed in 1924 and 1925. Meanwhile, General Steam chartered their sisters *Goldfinch* (226/1903) and *Bullfinch* (246/1903) to the new company, repainting their funnels from black to yellow with black top.

T. Small and Co. (Great Yarmouth) Ltd. continued to operate in their own right, and later in 1923 began services from Yarmouth to Antwerp and to Rotterdam. These were entitled the Norwich and Continental Steamship Services, as the bulk of the Antwerp traffic comprised steel and iron products for the factory of Boulton and Paul Ltd. in Norwich, the ships on the service sailing through to the inland town. The Rotterdam trade benefited from the export of cured herrings, these cargoes often being sent up the Rhine into Germany.

Amelia was built for Henry Newhouse but is seen here post-Second World War in the ownership of W. Cooper and Son, Kirkwall, who had her from 1920 until she was broken up at Charlestown in 1955. *[Graeme Somner]*

A summary of Great Yarmouth shipping services

Henry Newhouse and Co. (ABC Shipping Co. Ltd).
1894-1916

▼

Hull and Yarmouth Steamship Service
Cartwright, Wenn and Co. Ltd.
1919-1921
T. Small and Co. (Great Yarmouth) Ltd
1921-1923

▼

Great Yarmouth Shipping Co. Ltd.
General Steam Navigation Co. Ltd. 47%
1923-1931
General Steam Navigation Co. Ltd. 72%
1931-1946

Consolidation and modernisation

Growth in the continental services compensated for the decline in the original trade between Hull and Yarmouth, and this may have prompted a further reorganisation of Yarmouth's shipping services in 1931. Alongside its Hull service the Great Yarmouth company now absorbed Small's continental services and the London to Yarmouth trade of General Steam. The fleet was considerably augmented, with the transfer to the company of General Steam's *Goldfinch, Yellowhammer, Picardy* and *Peronne*, plus Small's steamers *Edith, Norwich Trader* and *Yarmouth Trader*. Small's aged *Saint Tudwal*, transferred from Henry Colville, had already been sold, and had probably been employed in tramp trades; for many years the Great Yarmouth company would send some its ships tramping.

At the very end of 1931 General Steam transferred to the Great Yarmouth Company its interests in Jas. Harborough and Son. Bought by General Steam in 1929, Harboroughs operated a considerable fleet of lighters, wherries and tugs on inland waterways. The company also took over the ABC Wharf at Yarmouth which had originally belonged to Newhouse, Crisp's Wharf at Lowestoft and General Steam's Baltic Wharf at Norwich (to the last named was transferred work from ABC's Norwich depot). These transfers of ships, smaller craft and other assets meant that General Steam now held 72% of the shares in the Great Yarmouth Shipping Co. Ltd. T. Small and Co. Ltd. now became a subsidiary, continuing with its ship broking and agency work at Yarmouth, and as Lloyd's agents.

Great Yarmouth Shipping now began a policy of gradually replacing its older steamers with new motor vessels,

Lowestoft Trader arriving in 1934 and the larger *Boston Trader* in 1936. Both were built by the Goole Shipbuilding and Repairing Co. Ltd. who were busy establishing a name for themselves as one of the few British coaster builders embracing the diesel engine. To match their names, *Goldfinch* became *Lynn Trader*, the names chosen acknowledging that calls at Boston and Kings Lynn had been added to the sailing schedules. It is probable that the remaining vessels not given 'Trader' names – *City of Malines, Picardy, Peronne* and *Yellowhammer* – were mainly sent tramping or were chartered out. The company's board minutes from October 1938 record that the *Yellowhammer* spent at least 12 months on charter to Colmans of Norwich, presumably not always carrying cargoes of their mustard. Ships were also supplied to parent company General Steam for its London to Grimsby service.

The company, or probably its subsidiary T. Small and Co. Ltd., acted as agents for Soviet ships using Yarmouth

Saint Tudwal was owned by associates of the Great Yarmouth company, and probably went tramping. She is seen at Preston (above). *[World Ship Society Ltd.]*

Bullfinch of 1903 was chartered by parent General Steam to the Great Yarmouth company. She is seen in General Steam colours passing Woolwich in February 1923. *[National Maritime Museum P28961]*

and Lynn, but it was increasingly annoyed by the USSR's unwillingness to pay its debts; by 1938 these amounted to £3,500. The seriousness of this to the company can be realised when this figure is compared with a profit of £8,172 for the year. Despite this, the company was able to pay an annual dividend of 5%.

Wartime

The services, ships, men and property of Great Yarmouth Shipping suffered considerably during the Second World War. Very soon after the outbreak of war, *Picardy* and *Yarmouth Trader* were requisitioned for government service, and other ships, lighters and river tugs followed. By June 1940 the company's regular services had all been closed, along with the Hull and Kings Lynn depots, and those ships which were still free of requisition were sent tramping. Annual profits were more or less halved during the war, probably because many of the company's ancillary activities had to be abandoned. Typical profits were £3,176 for the year ending June 1940, and £3,845 for 1945. Nevertheless, a consistent 5% dividend was declared.

On 9th February 1940 the company's newest vessel, *Boston Trader*, was bombed and set on fire by Luftwaffe aircraft and had to be beached on the north coast of Norfolk. Her master, Captain H.R. Brown, was put in charge of a successful refloating operation, and the *Boston Trader* returned to service on 9th August 1940. Brown subsequently became Marine Superintendent. The managed Dutch-built coaster *Empire Daffodil* was damaged by air attack south west of the Isle of Wight on 9th July 1940. She was taken to Portland and then to Southampton for repair.

Despite being damaged by a Luftwaffe bomb in 1940, *Boston Trader* completed 30 years' work for the company. *[Author's collection]*

Worse was to follow in 1942, with offices at Yarmouth rendered uninhabitable, store rooms in the town destroyed by fire, and two warehouses at Norwich totally destroyed. The major tragedy, however, was the mining of *Norwich Trader* off Harwich on 7th January 1942, the old steamer taking with her a crew of six and a gunner. The directors promised 'every assistance' to the men's dependants.

It is not clear from surviving records when the company ended the Yarmouth to Hull service, which was its original *raison d'etre* (board minutes from 1923 to 1938 have not survived). The depot at Hull (along with that at Kings Lynn) was closed in 1940, but just prior to the war the company was sending much of its cargo by road. After the Second World War board minutes do not refer to the Hull trade (nor to calls at Lowestoft or Kings Lynn), and it is likely that coastal services were simply not resumed in 1945.

To be continued

Fleet list (part 1)

1. CLANSMAN 1923-1924 Iron
O.N. 81960 265g 152n.
150.1 x 21.7 x 10.7 feet.
C. 2-cyl by John Rowan and Son Ltd., Belfast; 60 NHP.
1880: Built by Workman, Clark and Co. Ltd., Belfast (Yard No. 1) for Alexander McMullin, Ballymena, County Antrim as ETHEL.
12.1881: Sold to Compagnie Francaise, Paris, France and renamed OBOKH.
2.1883: Sold to Thomas Banks, London, registered at Swansea, and renamed ETHEL.
5.10.1885: Sold to David MacBrayne, Glasgow.
3.1.1906: Owners became David MacBrayne Ltd.
4.10.1910: Renamed CLANSMAN.
8.5.1916: Sold to Alexander F. Blackater, Glasgow.
21.5.1918: Sold to Peter S. Couper, Kirkwall.

15.1.1920: Sold to Arthur Middleton Gibson, Sunderland.
8.9.1920: Transferred to the Middleton Steam Ship Co. Ltd. (Arthur Middleton Gibson, manager), Newcastle-upon-Tyne.
25.11.1921: Sold by mortgagees to Frederick Spashett, Lowestoft.
11.1.1923: Transferred to T. Small and Co. (Great Yarmouth) Ltd. (Arthur H. Cartwright, manager), Great Yarmouth.
30.6.1923: Transferred to Great Yarmouth Shipping Co. Ltd., Yarmouth.
22.10.1924: Foundered in a severe gale about three miles north east of Haisboro' Light Vessel while on a voyage from Hull to Yarmouth with general cargo. The crew took to the boats, were picked up by the Cromer lifeboat and taken to Yarmouth.
16.12.1924: Register closed.

2. IVYTOWN 1924-1927
O.N. 115631 264g 104n.
142.5 x 21.3 x 10.5 feet.

C. 2-cyl. by A. Rodgers and Co., Glasgow.
4.1903: Completed by John Fullerton and Co., Paisley (Yard No.172).
24.4.1903: Registered in the ownership of the Frontier Town Steamship Co. Ltd. (Joseph Fisher, manager), Newry as ABBOT.
22.4.1915: Sold to Joseph Llewelyn and John T. Evans, Cardiff.
30.6.1915: Sold to the Care and Young Shipping Co. Ltd., Cardiff.
6.10.1916: Sold to William A. Jenkins and Co., Swansea.
23.12.1916: Sold to Ernest Wilford, London.
20.7.1917: Sold to Channel Transports Ltd. (Stone and Rolfe, managers), Llanelly.
30.8.1917: Sold to the Abbot Steamship Co. Ltd. (Robert A. Constantine and Thomas H. Donking, managers), Middlesbrough.
22.6.1918: Stone and Rolfe became managers.

Built for carrying coal across the Irish Sea, *Ivytown* worked for the company between 1924 and 1927. *[Author's collection]*

1.11.1918: Sold to Town Line (London) Ltd. (Harrison, Sons and Co., managers), London.
15.2.1919: Renamed IVYTOWN.
9.2.1924: Sold to Norman B. Leslie, Dundee.
12.12.1924: Acquired by the Great Yarmouth Shipping Co. Ltd., Yarmouth.
22.2.1927: Sold to Arthur Ogg, Aberdeen.
4.1.1929: Sold to Steam Coasters Ltd. (Alfred B. Wade, manager), Cardiff.
2.7.1934: Sold to Arthur Simpson (Comben, Longstaff and Co. Ltd., managers), London.
4.1935: Sold to J.N. Vlassopoulos, Greece and renamed BALTIKI.
29.7.1935: Registered in the ownership of the Brook Shipping Co. Ltd. (Comben, Longstaff and Co. Ltd., managers), London as KENTBROOK.
27.12.1935: Left Plymouth for Portsmouth with a cargo of stone and disappeared.
12.10.1936: Register closed.

3. CITY OF MALINES 1925-1946
O.N. 123657 373g 150n.
135.0 x 23.6 x 11.9 feet.
T. 3-cyl. by MacColl and Pollock Ltd., Sunderland; 78 NHP, 425 IHP, 10 knots.
21.4.1905: Launched by Mackay Brothers, Alloa (Yard No. 1).
5.1905: Completed.
11.6.1906: Registered in the ownership

of the Anglo-Belgian Prince Line Ltd (Thomas Ellis, manager), London as PRINCE LEOPOLD.
19.6.1913: Sold to the Brussels Steamship Co. Ltd. (Walter L. Thomas, manager), London.
25.2.1920: Renamed CITY OF MALINES.
21.12.1925: Acquired by the Great Yarmouth Shipping Co. Ltd., Great Yarmouth.
22.7.1946: Sold to T. and W. Colassi Ltd., London for £5,000.

10.10.1947: Sold to the Wirral Shipping Co. Ltd. (Henry Elmer, manager), London.
12.1.1948: Renamed WIRRAL BANK.
19.2.1948: Transferred to the Wirral Steamship Co. Ltd. (Henry Elmer, manager), London.
25.1.1951: Sold by the Midland Bank to Norman Dakin, London.
15.5.1951: Renamed SEGURA.
22.6.1952: Breaking up began by T.W. Ward Ltd. at Grays, Essex.
20.5.1953: Register closed.

City of Malines was unusual for such a small coaster in having her engines amidships. She was photographed as *Wirral Bank*, with a damaged stem, in the Thames during April 1951 towards the end of her career. *[Author's collection]*

4. GOLDFINCH/LYNN TRADER
1931-1951
O.N. 160039 337g 122n.
130.8 x 23.6 x 9.5 feet.
T. 3-cyl. by W.J. Yarwood and Sons Ltd., Northwich; 53 NHP.
11.12.1926: Launched by W.J. Yarwood and Sons Ltd., Northwich (Yard No. 287).
27.4.1927: Completed.
27.4.1927: Registered in the ownership of Henry Leetham and Sons Ltd. (Herbert W. Holroyd, manager), York as VIVONIA.
1929: Sold to the General Steam Navigation Co. Ltd., London and renamed GOLDFINCH.
1931: Transferred to the Great Yarmouth Shipping Co. Ltd. (Henry I. Colville, manager), Great Yarmouth.
1936: Renamed LYNN TRADER.
1951: Sold to A.H. Tucker, Cardiff, renamed IMOGEN and converted to a sand suction dredger.
1.6.1964: Breaking up began by Haulbowline Industries Ltd., Passage West, Cork.
6.1964: Register closed.

5. YELLOWHAMMER   1931-1947
O.N. 149969 217g 84n.
119.2 x 21.1 x 8.7 feet.
C. 2-cyl. by Crabtree and Co. Ltd. Great Yarmouth; 35 NHP, 275 IHP, 8.5 knots.
1960: Oil engine 2SCSA 4-cyl. by Alpha-Diesel A/S, Fredrikshavn; 200 BHP, 8 knots.
30.12.1927: Registered in the ownership of the General Steam Navigation Co. Ltd., London as ROBIN.
1.1928: Completed by Crabtree and Co. Ltd. Great Yarmouth (Yard No. 185).
19.6.1929: Renamed YELLOWHAMMER.
14.12.1931: Transferred to the Great Yarmouth Shipping Co. Ltd., Yarmouth.
27.10.1947: Sold to W.N. Lindsay Ltd., Leith for £11,500.
23.2.1948: Renamed LINDEAN.

Vivonia in her builders' yard at Northwich awaiting completion for her York-based owners (top) and as *Lynn Trader* sailing from Great Yarmouth (middle) some time after transfer to the company and renaming in 1936. *[Both: Clive Guthrie collection]*

In 1951 *Lynn Trader* was sold to Cardiff owners and converted to a sand sucker, the fate of a number of ageing steam coasters. She was photographed as *Imogen* in July 1960 (bottom). *[J. and M. Clarkson]*

29.6.1948: Sold to Francis W. Henry, ship repairer, Leith.

28.10.1948: Sold to the Lindean Steamship Co. Ltd., Edinburgh (George D. Dow, Leith, manager).

23.5.1953: Register closed on sale to C.P. Jensen, Rudkobing, Denmark and renamed BIBE.

1968: Sold to Rudolf Sorensen, Odense, Denmark.

1972: Sold to Roger O.V. Carlsson, Stockholm, Sweden.

1975: Renamed NOMAD.

1977: Sold to Max Serras and Michael Tremayne Forshaw, St George's, Grenada and renamed LINDEAN under the St. Vincent flag.

1992: Deleted from 'Lloyd's Register' as continued existence in doubt.

6. PICARDY 1931-1950

O.N. 144421 320g 133n.
130.0 x 23.2 x 9.5 feet.
C. 2-cyl. by Crabtree and Co. Ltd., Great Yarmouth; 45 NHP, 360 IHP, 9 knots.

3.1920: Completed by Crabtree and Co. Ltd., Great Yarmouth (Yard No.177).

1.3.1920: Registered in the ownership of R. and J. Park Ltd., London as PICARDY.

7.5.1923: Sold to the General Steam Navigation Co. Ltd., London.

14.12.1931: Transferred to the Great Yarmouth Shipping Co. Ltd., Yarmouth.

1950: Sold to Barlow and Co. (Dundee) Ltd., Dundee.

1953: Renamed EDITH.

18.1.1966: Arrived at St. David's on Forth to be broken up by James A. White and Co. Ltd.

7. EDITH 1931-1936

O.N. 99488 148g 78n.
95.3 x 20.1 x 7.6 feet.
26.11.1914: 181g 98n 113.0 x 20.1 x 7.6 feet.
C. 2-cyl. by Alexander Hall and Co., Aberdeen; 30 NHP, 180 IHP, 8 knots.

7.1893: Completed by Alexander Hall and Co., Aberdeen (Yard No. 348).

26.7.1893: Registered in the ownership of Robert Rix and Sons, Hull as EDITH.

1.10.1917: Sold to Oakley, Sollas and Co. Ltd., London.

18.12.1917: Owners became the Olwen Steamship Co. Ltd. (Samuel W. Oakley, manager), London.

17.5.1921: Owners became Isaac and Louis Kahn, London.

26.7.1923: Sold to Henry Hillcoat, Norwich.

The camera-shy *Yellowhammer* is seen as *Lindean* during her brief Lindsey ownership, driven on to the wrong side of the breakwater at Macduff in April 1948. Surprisingly, she was salvaged and returned to service. *[Douglas J. Lindsay collection]*

Another transfer from General Steam was the Yarmouth-built *Picardy*, seen with a deck cargo of early containers or possibly crates. *[World Ship Society Ltd.]*

Edith aground during her Rix ownership. *[Rix Archives]*

Norwich Trader, probably in Dutch waters. Mined in January 1942 and sunk with her entire complement, she was the Great Yarmouth company's most serious casualty. *[Martin Lindenborn]*

18.3.1924: Sold to T. Small and Co. (Great Yarmouth) Ltd., Great Yarmouth.
17.12.1931: Acquired by the Great Yarmouth Shipping Co. Ltd. (Henry I. Colville, manager), Great Yarmouth.
9.7.1936: Sold to Joseph Barlow (36/64) and John Sinclair (28/64), Dundee trading as Barlow and Co. (Joseph Barlow, manager), Dundee.
6.1951: Broken up at Bo'ness.
20.9.1952: Register closed.

8. NORWICH TRADER (1) 1931-1942

O.N. 125752 217g 81n.
115.2 x 22.1 x 8.1 feet.
C. 2-cyl. by Crabtree and Co. Ltd., Great Yarmouth; 8½ knots.
12.10.1908: Launched by Cochrane and Sons, Selby (Yard No. 444).
2.1.1909: Registered in the ownership of Joseph H. Beckwith, trading as Beckwith and Co., Colchester as ESPERANTO.
5.3.1915: Sold to Griffith Davies, William O. Roberts and Thomas L. Roberts, Liverpool.
5.4.1915: Transferred to the Esperanto Steamship Co. Ltd. (Robert Owen and Co., managers), Liverpool.
16.4.1918: In collision with the steamer COLLIN (287/1915) which sank off Maughold Head, Ramsey, Isle of Man.
2.10.1919: Sold to William J. Kelly, Belfast.

29.12.1923: Sold to James Downey and Patrick Neville, Dublin.
4.3.1925: Sold to Frederick W. Taylor, Sunderland.
9.4.1925: Renamed ELEMORE.
9.3.1927: Sold to T. Small and Co. (Great Yarmouth) Ltd., Yarmouth.
14.4.1927: Renamed NORWICH TRADER.
17.12.1931: Transferred to the Great Yarmouth Shipping Co. Ltd., Yarmouth.
7.1.1942: Mined and sunk in position 51.55.07 north by 01.32.05 east whilst on a voyage from London to Yarmouth

with general cargo. Her crew of six and one D.E.M.S. gunner were lost.
1943: Wreck dispersed.

9. YARMOUTH TRADER (1) 1931-1946

O.N. 143512 312g 125n.
130.0 x 23.2 x 9.5 feet.
C. 2-cyl. by Crabtree and Co. Ltd., Great Yarmouth; 45 NHP, 360 IHP, 9 knots.
4.1917: Launched by Crabtree and Co. Ltd., Great Yarmouth (Yard No. 178).
7.1920: Completed.

The locally-built *Yarmouth Trader* ended her days as the *Ben Jee* and is seen above in the Mersey in July 1951, a few months before a stranding in the Isle of Man left her a constructive total loss. *[J. and M. Clarkson collection]*

19.7.1920: Registered in the ownership of the Elveden Shipping Co. Ltd. (Griffin Brothers, managers), Cardiff as STERTPOINT.

31.5.1921: Sold to Arthur W. Page (David L. MacIntosh, manager), Bristol.

29.12.1926: Sold to Isaac W. Laing, Sunderland.

10.3.1927: Renamed ASHDENE.

17.12.1928: Sold to Frederic W. Gibson, Sunderland.

20.1.1930: Sold to T. Small and Co. (Great Yarmouth) Ltd., Yarmouth.

8.2.1930: Renamed YARMOUTH TRADER.

17.12.1931: Transferred to the Great Yarmouth Shipping Co. Ltd., Yarmouth.

21.10.1946: Sold to the Ramsey Steamship Co. Ltd., Ramsey for £7,250.

14.1.1947: Renamed BEN JEE.

20.11.1952: Stranded half a mile south of the Point of Ayre, Isle of Man whilst on a voyage from Carrickfergus to Garston in ballast.

16.12.1952: Refloated and taken to Ramsey Harbour.

2.1.1953: Arrived at Birkenhead to await dry-docking.

19.2.1953: Arrived at Preston for breaking up by T.W. Ward Ltd.

27.6.1953: Register closed.

10. PERONNE 1932-1946
O.N. 1432285 207g 122n.
99.8 x 21.7 x 10.3 feet.

Peronne passing Woolwich on 8th May 1937. *[National Maritime Museum P12342]*

C. 2-cyl. by W.J. Yarwood and Sons Ltd., Northwich.

28.6.1917: Launched by W.J. Yarwood and Sons Ltd., Northwich (Yard No. 244).

31.1.1918: Completed for R. and J. Park Ltd., London as PERONNE.

1922: Sold to the General Steam Navigation Co. Ltd., London.

1932: Transferred to the Great Yarmouth Shipping Co. Ltd., Yarmouth.

1946: Sold to the Tay Sand Co. Ltd. (J. Neilson, manager), Dundee for £3,000.

4.6.1960: Arrived at Charlestown, Fife to be broken up by Shipbreaking Industries Ltd.

7.6.1960: Breaking up began.

11. LOWESTOFT TRADER 1934-1961
O.N. 164156 311g 149n.
130.7 x 24.6 x 9.0 feet.
2SCSA 5-cyl. oil engine by British Auxiliaries Ltd., Glasgow; 8½ knots.

11.10.1934: Launched by the Goole Shipbuilding and Repairing Co. (1927)

Lowestoft Trader, the first of only two ships actually built for the Great Yarmouth company. *[World Ship Society Ltd.]*

Ltd., Goole (Yard No. 305).
12.1934: Completed for the Great
Yarmouth Shipping Co. Ltd., Great
Yarmouth as LOWESTOFT TRADER.
6.11.1961: Sold to the Channel Shipping
Co. Ltd., Jersey for £5,500 and renamed
PONTAC.
1962: Sold to Nicolaos Zoulias and
Nicolaos Ninos, Piraeus, Greece and
renamed MILOS.
1964: Sold to G. and A.D. Andrias
and others, Piraeus and renamed
VASSILIOS LITOCHORON.
1973: Sold to N. Perris, Piraeus.
1977: Sold to Kefal Navigation Co.
Ltd., Limassol, Cyprus.
1979: Renamed SAN ANTONIO.
10.1985: Deleted from 'Lloyd's
Register' as continued existence in
doubt.

12. BOSTON TRADER 1936-1962
O.N. 164171 381g 176n.
143.5 x 26.2 x 8.9 feet.
2SCSA 6-cyl oil engine. by British
Auxiliaries Ltd., Glasgow; 9 knots.
31.10.1936: Launched by the Goole
Shipbuilding and Repairing Co. Ltd.,
Goole (Yard No. 320).
11.1936: Completed for the Great
Yarmouth Shipping Co. Ltd., Yarmouth
as BOSTON TRADER.
1962: Sold to Captain Euclid Bonchard,
St. Francois, Quebec, Canada for

Boston Trader at anchor in the Thames. She was a modestly enlarged version of
the *Lowestoft Trader*. [World Ship Society Ltd.]

£20,000 and renamed MONROE.
1964: Registered under the ownership
of E. Bouchard Ltd. and renamed
ELISE MARIE.
1966: Sold to B. Labelle, Quebec and
renamed SONIA D.
1970: Sold to Lary Maritime Transport,
Quebec
1972: Sold to Transports Maritimes

Vigneault B., Quebec (Havre St. Pierre)
and renamed VIGNAULT B.
2. 12.1972: Struck wharf, broke
moorings and sank in heavy weather at
Sainte Anne des Monts. Subsequently
refloated but sank in a gale while under
tow, 12 miles east of Les Mechins.

To be continued

SOURCES AND ACKNOWLEDGEMENTS

We thank all who gave permission for their photographs to be used,
and for help in finding photographs we are particularly grateful
to Tony Smith, Jim McFaul and David Whiteside of the World
Ship Photo Library; to Malcolm Cranfield, Ian Farquhar, F.W.
Hawks, Peter Newall, Russell Priest, William Schell; and to David
Hodge and Bob Todd of the National Maritime Museum, and other
museums and institutions listed.

      Research sources have included the Registers of
William Schell and Tony Starke, 'Lloyd's Register', 'Lloyd's
Confidential Index', 'Lloyd's Shipping Index', 'Lloyd's War
Losses', 'Mercantile Navy Lists', 'Marine News', 'Sea Breezes'
and 'Shipbuilding and Shipping Record'. Use of the facilities of the
World Ship Society, the Guildhall Library, the National Archives
and Lloyd's Register of Shipping. Particular thanks also to Heather
Fenton for editorial and indexing work, and to Marion Clarkson for
accountancy services.

Great Yarmouth Shipping Co. Ltd.
The author is particularly grateful to Alan Faulkner who identified the
most important documents which were used to research this feature.
The major sources are records of the General Steam Navigation
Co. Ltd. on loan to the National Maritime Museum, Greenwich,
GSN25/4, GSN/25/5 and GSN/25/12. Also consulted were GSN
Newsletter No. 106; Mike Stammers 'Tugs on the 'Norwich River'
– a personal reminiscence' *Waterways Journal*, **15**, 2013, pages
5-9; and N. Robins *Birds of the Sea: 150 years of the General Steam
Navigation Company*, Bernard McCall, Portishead, 2007.

Aberdeen Steam Twilight and South West Scenes: Fowey
Thanks to John Bartlett, of the World Ship Society's Central
Record, for providing background information on some of the ships
mentioned in these articles.

Talbot-Booths
The editors are grateful to David Greenman for reading and
commenting on a draft of this article and providing details of the
dates of 'Janes's Merchant Ships'. Many of the books mentioned
have been examined in various libraries and identified through
booksellers' catalogues.

The tussle for the 'circular saw'
This article originally appeared in 'New Zealand Marine News'
volume 49, number 2 (2000) and is reproduced with the kind
permission of the publisher.

Clarendon Dock, Belfast
'The Irish Sword', Journal of the Military History Society of
Ireland, Volume XVI, no. 62, 1984, has a very detailed account of
Sean MacBride and the *St. George* by Michael MacEvilly.

British Phosphate Commission charters
In addition to WSS books on Hogarth, Lyle and Bank Line, the editors
consulted 'From Cape to Cape: the History of Lyle Shipping' by John
Orbell, Edwin Green and Michael Moss (Paul Harris, Edinburgh, 1978),
an exemplary business history which does full justice to Lyle's ships

CLARENDON DOCK, BELFAST
Ian Wilson

This photograph is a gift that keeps on giving. There are numerous photographs of ships in Belfast, but few if any which capture an event like this. A crowd is standing on a Royal Navy motor launch on what seems to be a dank, cold, winter's day. Everyday labour in the port continues: a puffer unloads bagged cargo with her steam winch and derrick. A sailing ship is alongside the launch. What is going on?

It seems we are seeing an auction, probably of the launch, and I think I know who a prospective buyer is. The burly man to the right of the auctioneer with his left hand on the derrick has been identified as Samuel Gray, one of the best-known (some would say notorious) characters in Belfast's 'Sailortown' in the 1920s and 30s. Stevedore, shipowner, salvage contractor and city councillor, Gray bought and sold small ships with great regularity. Some were bought as casualties, refloated and sold, some were coastal steamers with which he traded, others were tugs, former Guinness Liffey barges, salvage steamers and even (at the height of his ambitions) the former Blackpool excursion paddler *Greyhound*, for the operation of which on Belfast Lough he formed the Abercorn Steamship Co. Ltd. in 1923. There are those (indeed, more than a few) who would allege Gray induced skippers to lose steamers deliberately for insurance purposes, and question marks have hung over the circumstances of fates including the *Stramore*, *Bangor* and *Texa*. (I tentatively asked his grand-daughter about this and she laughed 'it sounds just like him'!)

But here it seems Gray is interested in one of the 580 motor launches ordered from the Elco firm in New Jersey for the massive inshore needs of Britain in the war. They were then sold off for sums averaging £400, and today only one is believed to exist, as a wreck on the upper reaches of the Thames. (There is a terrific website dedicated to these interesting vessels, www.motorlaunchpatrol.net)

Is there any way of identifying this unit? Probably not, but there is a tantalising chance it may be ML 476, which is known to have been in Belfast. The full story of its subsequent adventures did

not become known for 60 years. A Lieutenant John Swift bought it for £200 in 1924 from Messrs. Lindsey, Belfast linen merchants. But this was not his real name. He was young Sean MacBride of the IRA and he was planning to pick up escaping internees. The break-out was aborted, and on the way south to Dun Laoghaire the *St. George* – MacBride had cheekily renamed her with a thoroughly English name – was wrecked in Dundrum Bay. MacBride was to go on to be a Nobel Peace Prize winner, was a founder of Amnesty International, and his descendants still have the binnacle and compass retrieved from the wreck.

The sailing ship's name can just be made out – *Falcon*. She was a wooden schooner built by Nicholson of Glasson Dock in 1894 for pilot duties at Fleetwood, and was acquired by Belfast Harbour Commissioners for similar use. A harbour policeman watches warily from the deck. (At this distance in time I feel safe enough saying the two characters on the far side of the lifeboat do look a bit shady...) No name is visible on the puffer which is probably one of Hay's, possibly delivering bagged cement from Magheramorne in Larne Lough. This shed was used until about 1980; coasters up to 50 metres or so being able to enter the dock from the River Lagan – but now there are very few coasters under 80 metres!

Nowadays Clarendon Dock, which dates from 1850, is surrounded by 'urban regeneration' as the port has developed seawards, but the important early graving dock begun in 1796 has been preserved, its entrance being just to the left of the scene here.

This is a marvellous glimpse of a moment in time, with the cast of characters caught naturally, and offering what must be rare detail of the deck and fittings of a First World War motor launch. But disposal records of the huge fleet are very sketchy, and we'll probably never know if Sam Gray concluded the purchase. A large number of these vessels became lovingly-maintained private pleasure craft, but if Sam Gray did buy her, it was just another day, another deal!

[Courtesy of Albert Ferran]

SOUTH WEST SCENES
3. Fowey

Fowey.

Still seeing shipping today, Fowey has been both a major port for loading china clay, copper and tin ores and has also provided lay-up berths for idle ships.

Hall Walk was a very popular viewpoint for the Victorian photographer. The Frith postcard above includes mainly sailing vessels, with two small steamers in the distance – probably tugs – and at least one steam yacht, dressed overall for a regatta. The commercial sailing vessels in the foreground are mainly Scandinavian judging by their large deckhouses. They will have brought timber to ports in the south west and will be waiting to load, probably at Par. Left to right they are a three-masted schooner, a barquentine, a topsail schooner - probably British - a grey-hulled brigantine and another barquentine.

The postcard view below includes two further steamers, the central one probably belonging to Furness, Withy, frequent visitors to Fowey. *[Editors' collections]*

Looking inland from the viewpoint of Hall Walk, the postcard above is entitled 'Fowey River at Mixtow' and shows at least seven sailing vessels, varying in size from a ketch (right), through a brig (left background), several three-masted schooners (nearest camera, and middle background) to a substantial barquentine (furthest left). Subsequent photos show how the western bank of the Fowey River, in particular, has been developed.

There are at least ten sail or steam vessels in the postcard view of the china clay jetties below, yet identifying them has proved frustrating. Just to the right of the middle is a Doxford Turret with a letter A on her funnel and a short name, but no obvious candidates can be found in John Lingwood's book on the type.

Two other names can be read. The large steamer to the right of the Turret is *Liberia*, but her black funnel with two white bands does not fit with any of the known vessels of this name. To the extreme right is a small steamer named *Cuba*, but which of several of the name is not known. *[Both: J. and M. Clarkson collection]*

Furthest from the camera is Furness, Withy's *Pennine Range* (above). Built by J. L. Thompson and Sons Ltd., Sunderland in 1903 for the Neptune Steam Navigation Co. Ltd., she was sold to Seagers of Cardiff as *Darius* in 1915, and torpedoed two years later.

The nearest steamer is *Figaro*, a coaster built in 1907 by the Williamson brothers at Workington for their own account as *Voreda*, and sold to owners in Rouen who renamed her *Figaro* in 1912. She was mined in January 1918.

Beyond her, the nearest of the two steamers moored in the harbour undoubtedly belongs to Richard Hughes of Liverpool: her funnel has his raised red band. Hughes' 'Rose boats' were such frequent visitors to the china clay tips at Fowey that their owner had, not just an office there, but also a fleet of railway wagons to bring china clay from the workings. The first name is only four letters long and, given the date just before the First World War, is probably *Pink Rose* of 1891, which closely matches a photograph of her. It could also be *Wild Rose* of 1888 of which no photograph is known. These were lost, respectively, in 1917 and 1919. *[Roy Fenton collection]*

Although the 19th century steamer in the foreground cannot be identified (below), this Valentine's post card offers a good perspective on Fowey's landward facilities, particularly the rail connections. Note the wagon turntable, and china clay everywhere. *[J. and M. Clarkson collection]*

The peaceful view of Fowey above with the steamer *Blairlogie* in the foreground is dated 24th November 1926, a date born out by the condition of the trees in the background, only some of which have lost their leaves. In what were depressed times, *Blairlogie* appears to be waiting to load rather than being laid up, as coal smoke drifts from her funnel and a small cloud of steam from a winch by her mainmast.

Blairlogie's owners were the Clydesdale Navigation Co. Ltd., managed by G. Nisbet and Co. of Glasgow, and she is unusual for a British steam tramp in having been built and engined by Rotterdam Droogdok Maatschappij. She was completed in 1912 for Dutch owners as *Oostdijk*, being bought by the Glasgow company and renamed in 1922. Sale to Finnish owners in 1936 saw her renamed *Agnes*. She was sunk by the Soviet submarine *ŠČ-406* in the Baltic on 1st November 1942. *[Roy Fenton collection]*

The appearance of the photograph below on E-bay brought joy to an editor's heart, as no other photographs are known of this steam coaster. She began life at S. McKnight's yard at Ayr in 1890 as *Burnock*, one of a pair built for local company David Rowan and Walter Bain (her sister was *Garnock*). From about 1890, Rowan and Bain managed the Ayr Steam Shipping Co. Ltd. Established about 1875, its services included passengers and cargo from Ayr to Larne, Belfast and Campbeltown; and Kingston Dock, Glasgow to Barrow. In May 1908 the company came under the control of Laird Line, and was absorbed in 1921.

Sold in 1899, nine changes of owner ensued for *Burnock*, and three renamings: to *Temaire* in 1915, *Innisholm* in 1921, and *Austin Gough* in 1927. The last of these saw *Austin Gough* owned by Gough's General Distributing Co. Ltd. of Southampton. In 1931, following a further brief sale, she was broken up. *[J. and M. Clarkson collection]*

Thomas Coppack's steam coaster *Watergate* loads china clay on 7th July 1932 (above). The well-known Connah's Quay ship owner, manager and agent had bought the 1912 Dublin-built steamer from Spillers late in 1927 as *Wheatlands*, but waited until 1929 before renaming her. Coppack's fleet of steam and motor coasters almost invariably had plain yellow funnels with black tops, but *Watergate* was probably unique in having a elegant, cursive letter 'C' in black on the yellow.

Watergate had an eventful wartime career. In 1940 she is reputed to have been the last ship to leave Brest before it was occupied, and in 1944 was

one of many coasters to take part in the Normandy landings. She was damaged on the beach at Arromanches, but was thoroughly repaired, to the extent that Coppacks could find a buyer for her in 1947, and she steamed on for a Southampton-based owner until broken up at Llanelly in 1953. *[R.Stimson/J. and M. Clarkson]*

Another coaster owned in the north west, *Edern* (466/1920) has the honour of inaugurating a new jetty for the Great Western Railway (below). *Edern* was owned by the wonderfully-named Manchester, Liverpool and North Wales Steamship Co. Ltd. The moving

spirit behind this venture was Rear Admiral John Parry Jones-Parry, who was born in the village of Edern on the Llyn peninsula.

Built for the company by Cochrane and Sons at Selby, *Edern* was managed by Robert R. Clark, also of Liverpool. In 1932 transfer to Clark's own company, the Overton Steamship Co. Ltd., saw her lose the splendid crossed battleaxes emblem on her funnel in favour of a more prosaic yellow with blue letter 'O'. Clark sold her in 1942, and after three changes of owner and one new name, *Warren Chase* in 1946, she was broken up at Gateshead in 1954. *[Roy Fenton collection]*

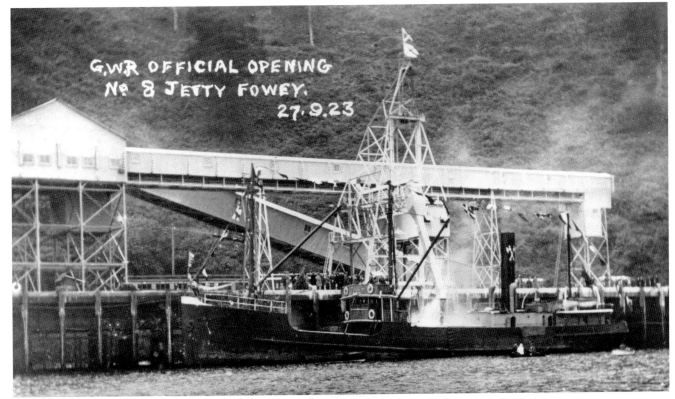

Jetties, Fowey.

Another of Richard Hughes coasters is seen from the same viewpoint as an earlier photograph. In Hughes' fleet, four large steamers were particularly distinctive, with two masts to serve the two holds ahead of the bridge and two masts to serve the single hold aft. All were completed by John Fullerton and Co. at Paisley between 1920 and 1922 and given names of Allied commanders during the First World War, with Hughes' 'Rose' suffix. Tantalisingly, the name on the stern of this example at anchor in the harbour is not quite readable, but appears to consist of two four-letter words, so could be either *Haig Rose* (1,177/1920) or *Foch Rose* (1,135/1922). The former was an early war loss, posted missing on 11th December 1940 after leaving Barry for Plymouth with coal. *Foch Rose* survived the war, gaining a wheelhouse during the conflict, and steaming on until broken up at Blyth in 1956. The fourth mast in these ships seems to have been unnecessary; *Haig Rose* losing hers before her disappearance and *Foch Rose* and *Jellicoe Rose* not retaining theirs after the war. *[J. and M. Clarkson collection]*

With a name reminiscent of one of Tolkein's dwarves, the Norwegian *Gimle* waits to load china clay. The small steamer had been built for Norway in 1916 by a Dutch yard, Jonker & Stans at Hendrik-Ido-Ambacht, as *Froland*. At the time British yards, who would almost inevitably have built such a vessel prewar, were unable to accept overseas orders, to the great benefit of yards in the neutral Netherlands. She briefly carried the name *Troldholden* before becoming *Gimle* in 1919. Yet another war loss, the neutral ship paid the price of trading with Britain on 4th December 1939 when torpedoed and sunk by *U 31* in the North Sea after leaving Hartlepool with coke for Gothenburg. *[R.Stimson/J. and M. Clarkson]*

Ships laid up at Fowey were moored in trots of those of individual companies, so that a small crew of shipkeepers could do something towards looking after them all. Three owned by companies in the Strick group appear in this view, including *Medjerda* of 1924 and *Thala* of 1928. Both would return to trade, but both became war losses within weeks of each other whilst bringing iron ore from Pepel to the Tees. The Gray-built *Medjerda*, owned by the La Tunisienne Steam Navigation Co. Ltd., survived until sunk with all hands by *U 105* on 18th March 1941. The previous month, on 8th February 1941, the Readhead-built *Thala* owned by Cory and Strick (Steamers) Ltd. had piled up on South Uist in the Outer Hebrides. *[R.Stimson/J. and M. Clarkson]*

A rather dreary 17th April 1933, the gloom accentuated by the sight of three of John Cory's tramps laid up at Fowey at the depth of the interwar depression. Left to right they are *Reading* of 1914, *Ruperra* of 1925 and *Ravenshoe* of 1916.

The last-named was bought by one of John Cory's companies in 1922, having been built at West Hartlepool for local owners as *Kepwickhall*, and

having had a brief career with a Cardiff owner as *Marnetown*. *Ravenshoe* is unlikely to have sailed again for the Cardiff owner: in 1934 she was bought by Greek owners and renamed *Elengo A. Kydoniefs*. She was wrecked off Cape Verde on 12th April 1939, whilst on a voyage from Buenos Aires to Amsterdam with grain.

Reading was also sold to Greece in 1934, and only *Ruperra* was

put back into trade for Cory, until she was torpedoed and sunk in October 1940. The fleet of John Cory and Sons Ltd. seems never to have recovered from the twin blows of the depression and the Second World War, a conflict in which its three owned ships were lost. Although the company soldiered on until 1966, it was a shadow of its one-time self. *[R.Stimson/J. and M. Clarkson]*

China clay made a useful westbound cargo for the North Atlantic services of Bristol City Line of Steamships Ltd., and here their third *Bristol City* loads at Fowey in 1933. Built by the line's parent company, Charles Hill and Sons, at Bristol in 1920, she was sunk by *U 358* on 5th May 1943 whilst bound for New York in convoy ONS 5 with a cargo that included china clay. [Stimson/J. and M. Clarkson]

Another North Atlantic liner company which found it expeditious to load westbound cargoes of china clay was Head Line, operated by G. Heyn and Sons Ltd. of Belfast.

Fanad Head (5,200/1917) (opposite middle) and Torr Head (5,221/1923) (opposite bottom) were versions of the same design delivered by Heyn's local builders Workman, Clark and Co. Ltd., and both registered in the ownership of the Ulster Steamship Co. Ltd.

Fanad Head was a very early Second World War loss, captured and torpedoed in the North Atlantic by U 30 whilst sailing independently on 14th September 1939. Torr Head was an early sale, going in 1933 to Chilean owners to be renamed Alamo. As this she steamed on until broken up in Italy during 1960. [Both: J. and M. Clarkson collection]

Although Margay appears to be bound out from Fowey in this fine 1933 photograph (above), it is not a happy scene. She is quite evidently light rather than loaded with china clay, and is bound for Genoa and demolition, having been sold to Italian breakers in April 1933. Kaye, Son and Co. Ltd. had acquired and renamed her only in 1932, undoubtedly hoping for a bargain as she was under arrest by the Admiralty Marshall as the Greek Christoforos. She had been built on the Tyne in 1910 as Cape Transport for a Houlder Brothers' subsidiary, which had sold her to Greece in 1929. [R.Stimson/J. and M. Clarkson]

Fowey's geography has meant tugs have been essential for assisting the larger ships calling, although the Fowey Harbour Commissioners have favoured second-hand tugs, probably because their employment is fairly irregular.

The steam tug Tolbenny (124/1928) was built by Fellows, Great Yarmouth as F.T. Everard, and bought by the Fowey Tug Co. Ltd. in 1951 (below). Sold to Plymouth owners who renamed her Tactful in 1965, she was broken up at Plymouth in 1980. [J. and M. Clarkson]

The little *Cannis* (91/1953) (top, photographed in June 1971) was acquired in 1964 from the London & Rochester Trading Co. Ltd. who employed her as a lighterage tug under the name *Enticette*. The Thorne-built *Cannis* was sold away from Fowey in 1993 and after passing through several hands was acquired by owners in Bristol in 2002 and converted to a houseboat, with her Crossley Brothers engine removed. *[J. and M. Clarkson]*

Gribbin Head (132/1955) (middle) was the former *Ingleby Cross*, bought from theTees Towing Co. Ltd. in 1968. Built by Scott and Sons, Bowling she also had a Crossley engine. Sold by the Fowey Harbour Commissioners in 1990, she has since carried the names *Tuskar Rock* and *Triva II*. She may still be in existence although her current flag and owner are not known. *[J. and M. Clarkson collection]*

Tregeagle (213/1987) (bottom) was photographed on 9th August 1987. Built at Aberdeen, she was delivered to Clyde Shipping Ltd as *Flying Demon*, in 1984 moving across to the east of Scotland for Forth Tugs Ltd., Grangemouth as *Forth*. Fowey Harbour Commissioners bought and renamed her *Tregeagle* in 1986. Following sale to owners in Ireland during 2010 she retained her name, one of the editors being pleased to see her in Stromness during this summer, working for Foyle and Marine Dredging, according to details painted on her bridge wing. *[J. and M. Clarkson]*

In June 1971, the West German *Anna Rehder* (2,411/1965) waits to load at Fowey, attended by *Cannis*. She was built for Carsten Rehder, Hamburg by the Lindenau yard at Kiel (top). Sold to Greek owners as *Leslie* in 1973, she went missing on a voyage from Boulogne to Umm Said in March 1981. *[J. and M. Clarkson]*

To close, photographs of the Fowey River showing (above) the Bodinnick Ferry with in the background a motor coaster belonging to Rix of Hull, the Dutch-built *Bobrix* (647/1957) after lengthening in 1968. Below is a close up of the Bodinnick Ferry in June 1971, with a selection of contemporary British-built vehicles on board. In both photographs, note the motor boat alongside to provide propulsion for the ferry. *[Roy Fenton collection; J. and M. Clarkson]*

STEAM TWILIGHT AT ABERDEEN HARBOUR

Peter Myers

Among the more interesting ships which called at Aberdeen from 1964 to 1974, when I took a close interest in the harbour's shipping movements, were the traditional engines-amidships cargo steamers, which brought esparto grass and phosphate from North Africa, woodpulp, timber and general cargo from Scandinavia and pumice gravel from the Italian island of Lipari. They invariably had interesting histories and included some old-timers, not to mention one 1916-built steamer which had been converted to motor propulsion. They were also well-maintained, even those flying flags of convenience, but by today's standards they would be judged as uneconomic to operate because of the large crews needed to man them and their relatively high fuel consumption.

A visit to Aberdeen by the elderly steamer *Regulus* aroused more than usual interest at the port in 1955 because she had been the first ship built for the Aberdeen Coal Company back in 1902 when she was completed as the *Redhall* (884g) by Mackie and Thomson of Govan, Glasgow. Her Aberdeen owners had sold her in 1917 and she bore the names *Mildred Powell*, *Caroline* and *Regulus* before being renamed *Karoline* after being seized by the Germans at Bergen in 1940. She was recovered at Flensburg, being allocated as a war prize to Britain. She reverted to her previous name of *Regulus* and was managed for the Ministry of War Transport by the Springwell Shipping Co. Ltd. of London, before being sold in 1952 to Cia. Naviera Minores S.A., Costa Rica.

The *Regulus*, which arrived with timber, had a largely Estonian crew and one of her officers complimented her builders by saying she was made with much better material than they were putting into contemporary ships. During her Aberdeen ownership, one of her main claims to fame was that in October 1904 she loaded four 1,000-ton cargoes of coal in the Tyne for Aberdeen in eight days in contrast to her usual performance of two trips a week.

Within a few years of her Aberdeen visit her trading days came to an end when she was laid-up at Stockholm in January 1958, remaining there until

The Baltic steam tramp *Regulus* was originally the Aberdeen Coal Company's *Redhall* of 1902 and returned to her former home port in 1955 with a cargo of timber. *[William Schell]*

November 1959 when she arrived at Hemixen, Belgium, for breaking up.

Ten years later another cargo steamer, the *Nicos* (2,856g), attracted the interest of the local press when she arrived at Aberdeen from Algiers in 1965 with esparto grass for the city's paper mills. Eleven years earlier, in 1954, the *Nicos*, under a previous name of *Athenic* had cut a rather forlorn appearance as she lay moored to a buoy in the port's Victoria Dock. She was in fact the last ship owned by W.H. Cockerline and Co. Ltd. of Hull, and had been built as the *Empire Gareth* in 1943, one of 24 Scandinavian type tramp steamships built by William

Gray and Co. Ltd. of West Hartlepool. The *Athenic* lay idle at Aberdeen for nine months, occasionally breaking free from her moorings during gales, until she sailed on 23rd August 1954. As she passed through the upraised St Clement's Bridge she momentarily held up the royal car carrying the Duke of Edinburgh who had just disembarked from the Royal Yacht *Britannia*. Four months later, on 20th December, Cockerline sold the *Athenic* to owners registered in Panama and so ended the company's history as a ship owner which had begun in 1885.

The *Athenic* later bore the names *Astarte* and *Yanix* before

The *Nicos* of 1942, shown here under her previous name of *Astarte*, brought esparto grass from Algiers to Aberdeen in 1965. *[World Ship Society Ltd.]*

becoming the *Nicos* in 1961, being owned by Nicos Compania Navigazione S.A., of Beirut, and managed by A. Halcoussis and Co. of Greece. At Aberdeen, her master, Captain Christos Costis, described her as 'a fine sea-boat' and said she handled very well.

Another steamer which called at Aberdeen with esparto grass was the Panamanian-flagged *Arun* (2,002/1949) which visited the port in 1964. She was owned by Cia. Nav. 'Rasko', and had been built as the *Haro* by Oskarhamns Varv A/B, of Oskarshamn, Sweden. In 1965 she hoisted the Red Ensign after she became the *Kingham* of G.W. Thacker, Ltd. of Newcastle. She was no stranger to the Tyne as she had occasionally shipped coal from that river as the *Arun*. Imports of esparto grass were beginning to tail off when another Panamanian steamer, *Weston* (1,900g), discharged such a cargo at Blaikies Quay in January 1971. She had been built as the *Aun* in 1952 by Nylands Verksted, Oslo, for A/S Finn Johnsens Rederi of Bergen, Norway. She was renamed *Velox* in 1967 before becoming the *Weston* of Companhia Maritima Weston S.A. in 1970.

Esparto grass for making paper had been imported at Aberdeen from southern Spain and North Africa since the mid-19th century, and by 1907 imports into Scotland had reached about 125,000 tons annually. Esparto grass was steadily supplanted by woodpulp, and from 1885 the Aberdeenshire paper mill of Thomas Tait and Sons at Inverurie became one of the pioneers of using woodpulp, making their own pulp from Norwegian spruce rather than importing it. The Inverurie mill, along with the Aberdeen mills at Culter, Donside, Mugiemoss and Stoneywood, made a whole range of papers ranging from high-quality writing paper to paper used for packaging. Woodpulp from Scandinavia and latterly the United States continued to be one of the principal imports at Aberdeen harbour, but this has shrunk drastically following the contraction of the paper-making industry leaving Stoneywood as the last working mill in north-east Scotland.

One of the joys of Aberdeen harbour was that it was a mere five minutes' walk from the bus and railway stations so there was often time for a quick look to see if any interesting ships had arrived. Before getting the bus home one Sunday afternoon in November 1970 my sortie to Trinity

The Panamanian steamer *Arun* of 1954 called at Aberdeen in the summer of 1964 with esparto grass. *[Donald Rowell/Peter Myers collection]*

The *Weston* of 1952 brought esparto grass to Aberdeen in January 1971. *[Real Photographs Co. Ltd./Peter Myers collection]*

Quay was rewarded with the sight of the Norwegian motor ship *Ramsnes*, owned by Jens Hetland and Kaspar Nilsen, of Egersund, which had arrived with timber. Her hull lines betrayed a ship of much older vintage and she had been built as the cargo steamer *Falger* for Oslo owners by Trondhjems M/V, Trondheim in 1916, subsequently bearing the names *Akabahra* and *Mirva* before becoming the *Knoll* in 1939. She was in Britain when Norway was invaded by Germany in 1940 and later sailed in coastal and Atlantic convoys, being attacked several times by enemy aircraft. As related in 'Record 52', page 264, she was at Bari, Italy, in April 1945 when she was scuttled to prevent a fire on board spreading to her cargo of ammunition. She was later refloated and repaired and was converted to a motor ship in 1958. Almost a year after she called at Aberdeen, the *Ramsnes* grounded on 21st September 1971 at Drogsholmen while on a voyage from Moen to Shoreham. Although she was

refloated the same day she was declared a constructive total loss after an inspection at Haugesund and was towed to Dutch shipbreakers for demolition in 1972, so ending a remarkable 56-year career.

Timber for the construction industry was one of the staple imports at Aberdeen, much of it being imported by the firms of John Fleming and Co. Ltd. and George Gordon and Co. Ltd., the latter being bought by Fleming in 1959 although the two firms were run as separate businesses until May 1971. George Gordon had a sawmill and storage sheds at the east end of Blaikies Quay, but many will recall the stacks of timber that lined some of the harbour's quays and which were exposed to the elements.

John Fleming, which still exists, had moved their premises in 1903 from the Albert Sawmills at Albert Quay, Aberdeen harbour, to a site at St Clements, Footdee, just outwith the harbour estate. John Fleming, who was

Knoll in May 1959 after conversion to a motor ship. *[J. and M. Clarkson collection]*

The Hansa A type cargo steamer *Riazan* of 1944 visited Aberdeen in June 1972.
[J. and M. Clarkson]

The *Privodino* of 1957 brought pumice gravel from Lipari to Aberdeen in November 1971. *[J. and M. Clarkson]*

Lord Provost of Aberdeen between 1898 and 1902, was able to use his influence to rename Martin Avenue, beside his new premises, to Baltic Place, to reflect the origin of much of his imported timber.

As well as Baltic tramps such as the *Regulus* and *Ramsnes*, timber imports could also be seen stowed on the weather decks of Russian cargo steamers. One such ship which excited my interest in June 1972 was the *Riazan* (1,925g) of the Latvian Shipping Company, Riga, which lay at Regent Quay. Her tall funnel marked her out as a German wartime standard ship of the Hansa A type and was probably one of the few left still trading. She had been built in 1944 as the *Licentia* by Flensburger Schiffswerft-Gesellschaft, Flensburg, but after Germany's defeat in 1945 had been placed under the ownership of the British Ministry of War Transport, being renamed *Empire Gabon*. A year later the Allied Commission, which dealt with the allocation of seized enemy tonnage, passed her over to the USSR and she was renamed *Riazan*. Like most Soviet merchant ships of the period, she was well-maintained and belied her 28 years.

An example of the numerous B31 class of general cargo steamer/collier built for the Soviet Union by Stocznia Gdanska, Gdansk, was the *Privodino* (3,826/1957) of the Lithuanian Shipping Company, Klaipeda, which called at Aberdeen in November 1971. That year, David Fairhall, defence correspondent of the 'Guardian' newspaper, published his illuminating book, 'Russia Looks to the Sea, a study of the expansion of Soviet maritime power'. He revealed that the crews of Soviet cargo ships benefited from an elaborate system of incentive bonus payments awarded for increased productivity. A detailed comparison of the ship's planned targets and her actual performance was posted in the crew's quarters. Fairhall went on to add that the master of a timber carrier might be able to load more than his nominal cargo tonnage by loading only the absolute minimum of fuel oil and water and so achieve the profit target.

The *Privodino* had arrived from the Italian island of Lipari with pumice gravel, which was used for making breeze blocks and for which there would develop a huge demand throughout the 1970s in north-east Scotland. The increasingly affluent region enjoyed a building boom stimulated by the discovery and exploitation of North Sea oil and gas, a boom which also greatly benefited the timber trade.

Another Russian steamer, the *Balashov* (3,258/1955) of the Latvian Shipping Company, Riga, discharged flax at Regent Quay at the end of 1972 before sailing for Antwerp with the remainder of the cargo. She belonged to a class of 11 cargo steamers built by Neptun-Werft, Rostock in the mid-1950s for the Soviet Union and her flax cargo was destined for Richards and Co. Ltd., who had built up an extensive flax spinning, weaving and finishing works at its Broadford linen mill in Aberdeen. The mill was best known for the manufacture of canvas fire hoses, but now lies derelict although there are plans to convert it into flats.

The *Balashov*'s sister-ship *Kolpino* was still trading in the mid-1980s and was said to be the oldest steamer in Russia's Baltic merchant fleet. She was featured in Michael J. Kreiger's book 'Tramp' (1986) and he remarked that her officers' saloon could have belonged to a ship built in the 1930s even although the *Kolpino* dated from 1957.

Aberdeen was a popular port of call for Russian seafarers at that time as sightseeing tours of the city were organised for them by local man Alexander Macklin, who spoke fluent Russian and had acted as interpreter for Russian sailors since the mid-1950s. He was a veteran of the Battle of Jutland and had served with the Royal Navy during the Russian Civil War when Britain, the US, France and Japan had supported the White Russians against the Bolshevik Red Army.

Aberdeen's last coal-fired steam colliers, the *Mount Battock* (396/1939) and the *Thrift* (590/1931), had sailed for the breakers' yards in 1968, but just two years later the coal-burning cargo steamer *Puck* (1,200g) of the Polish Steamship Company aroused considerable interest at the port when she arrived with waste paper from Poland in September 1970. She had been built in 1949 by Swan, Hunter and Wigham Richardson Ltd. at Newcastle-upon-Tyne, and her propulsion machinery was a reciprocating steam engine with a low-pressure turbine. The *Puck*'s master, Captain Zozislaw Dutkiewice, told a local newspaper that his command was 'reliable at sea,

The Riga-registered *Balashov* of 1955 brought flax to Aberdeen in December 1972. This photograph was taken on 25th July 1973. *[Malcolm Cranfield]*

Mount Battock sailing from Aberdeen. Note the old control room in the background. *[J. and M. Clarkson collection]*

The coal-fired Polish steamer *Puck* of 1949 called at Aberdeen in September 1970 and December 1971. She is seen above sailing light from Goole on 11th May 1971. *[J. and M. Clarkson]*

The Polish motor ship *Elblag* of 1950 discharges timber at Upper Quay, Aberdeen on 11th October 1972 (left). She is seen again, with a black hull, in the Bristol Channel (right). *[Peter Myers; J. and M. Clarkson]*

quiet and pleasant in port'. He added that it was sometimes difficult to load the right grade of bunker coal, and that she had loaded extra bunkers in Poland, some of which was stowed on her boat deck. She returned to Aberdeen in December 1971 and the bits of coal lying on Waterloo Quay suggested she may have loaded bunkers there. This was one of her last commercial voyages as she arrived at Bruges, Belgium, for demolition on 14th January 1972.

Puck contrasted with another ship of the Polish Steamship Company which called at Aberdeen in October 1972. The *Elblag* (1,285/1950) was an attractive motor ship with engines amidships and had been built by Paul Lindenau Schiffswerft G.m.b.H. of

Memel. She discharged her timber cargo at Upper Quay, where, until four years earlier, the well-known *Thrift* had brought her coal shipments. The *Elblag* returned to Aberdeen a few months later, this time with waste paper from Gdynia which would be processed by the local paper mills.

Scottish Agricultural Industries imported large quantities of phosphate rock at Aberdeen as well as potash and basic slag for making compound fertilisers at its Sandilands works near Aberdeen beach. Most of the fertiliser was destined for the Scottish market, but occasional shipments were exported from Aberdeen to developing countries as part of Britain's overseas aid programme. They included shipments

to the Philippines by the Ben Line's *Benattow* (8,038/1951) in February 1975 and to Karachi in February 1977 by the Liberian-flag, Spanish-owned *Artagan* (8,067/1959), which was formerly Hogarth's *Baron Maclay*.

The imported phosphate arrived normally in bulk from Morocco and Senegal, but the veteran steamer *Sonja* brought hers in sacks when she arrived at Atlantic Wharf, Aberdeen, from Safi, Morocco, at the end of March 1973. The *Sonja* (1,569g) had been built by Helsingborg Varv. A/B of Helsingborg, Sweden, in 1940, for A/B Transmarin, also of that port. At Aberdeen she became the centre of a dispute after dockers claimed the bagged phosphate had been stowed

Benattow in the Thames, 25th February 1973. She loaded fertiliser at Aberdeen for the Philippines in 1975. *[J. and M. Clarkson]*

The *Sonja* of 1940 lies at Atlantic Wharf, Aberdeen on 26th March 1973 after arriving from Safi with phosphate. She called again at the port in late 1974, this time from Finland, being probably the last short-sea cargo steamer to visit Aberdeen. The Liberian-registered *Sonja* was a well-maintained ship which enjoyed a long career. *[Aberdeen Journals Ltd.]*

badly and was holding up the cargo's discharge. The dispute was settled after the Aberdeen Stevedoring Co. Ltd. offered the dockers bonuses on piece-time work and brought in extra men to help unload the cargo. The *Sonja*, which was owned by Compania Maritima Sonja S.A., Monrovia, was a typical Swedish cargo steamer of the period with a tall, black funnel abaft the wooden wheelhouse and bridge wings. She returned to Aberdeen towards the end of 1974, this time from Finland.

Another Swedish-built steamer to be made idle at Aberdeen because of industrial action was the Panamanian-registered *Vaigu* (1,978/1954), which was caught up in a national dock strike in August 1972. When the strike ended and she was able to finish discharging her cargo of woodpulp, my father, Ron, saw her sailing from Blaikies Quay during an expert display of ship-handling. A harbour boatman passed her hawser through the ring of one of the old mooring buoys in the Victoria Dock which then allowed the *Vaigu* to be warped round so that she was facing the entrance to the dock. Once the manoeuvre was completed, a couple of turns of her propeller enabled her to pass through the dock entrance and out into the Navigation Channel.

The *Vaigu,* which was owned by Companhia Maritima Virona S.A., Colon, Panama, and managed by John E. Sandstrom & Co. of Stockholm, had been built by Oskarshamns Varv. A/B, Oskarhamn, Sweden, as the *Nordanvik*, subsequently bearing the names *Gundel, Sinikka* and *Malla* before becoming the *Vaigu* in 1966. She was a typical Baltic tramp and returned to Aberdeen in October 1972 from Mantyluoto, Finland with woodpulp.

She was replaced on the woodpulp and general cargo run from the Baltic to Grangemouth and Aberdeen with the more economical motor ship *Becky* (1,792/1945) which was also owned by Companhia Maritima Virona S.A. She had, in fact, been named *Becky* when she was completed by Lindholmens,

The *Vaigu* of 1954 (left). Woodpulp from Mantyluoto, Finland is discharged from the *Vaigu* at Blaikies Quay, Aberdeen on 11th October 1972 (right). *[Peter Myers]*

The motor ship *Becky* of 1945 was a frequent visitor to Aberdeen between 1973 and 1975 with woodpulp and general cargo from Scandinavia. She is seen in the colours of her original owners, A/B Transmarin, colours she continued to wear for some time after her sale by Transmarin. *[J. and M. Clarkson]*

Gothenburg, for A/B Transmarin of Helsingborg, whose ships all had girls' names.

The *Becky* conjured up images of Scandinavia one evening in November 1973 at Blaikies Quay as snowflakes swirled around her funnel, illuminated by floodlights to allow the unloading of her woodpulp cargo. Several dockers had their parka hoods drawn up tightly against their chins, and they stamped their frozen feet on the bales of woodpulp already stacked up on the snow-covered quayside. The red glow from a brazier offered some welcome warmth on that bitterly cold night.

Seven months later a picture of the *Becky*'s bow looming menacingly over the road bridge over the River South Esk at Montrose appeared on the front page of a local newspaper. On 23rd June 1974, the *Becky* was sailing from the Angus port for Sweden when she was caught by the wind and tide which took her upstream. She dropped her port anchor which halted her just short of the bridge. As the tide eased she was swung round into the navigation channel with the help of two fishing boats and headed out to sea without any further trouble.

In November that year she arrived at Aberdeen, after calling at Methil, with woodpulp and general cargo. She was under the command

of Swedish shipmaster Captain Fritz Olsson, who although retired, was doing a two-month stint as relief master on the *Becky*. Aberdeen was a regular port of call for him when he commanded ships of the fondly remembered Monark Line of Stockholm.

The Monark Line was run by Arnold and Thomas de Champs and maintained a cargo liner service between Swedish and Finnish ports and Aberdeen and Grangemouth from the 1950s to the mid-1970s. The company's ships were immaculately turned out and always reminded me of scaled-down versions of Alfred Holt's Blue Funnel ships, although the blue was a darker shade. Their steamships included the *Monark* (1,599/1950), *Monodora* (1,350/1938), *Monarda* (1,524/1935), *Monita* (1,594/1950) and *Montrose* (2,054/1954). They were all second-hand purchases and their distinctive and individual profiles made them easily identifiable.

I first encountered the Monark Line in the summer of 1964 when I found the *Monodora* lying at Regent Quay, where the electric roof cranes of the granite-built Regent Sheds were discharging her cargo from Finland. The *Monodora* had been built as the *Tunisia* for Svenska Lloyd, Gothenburg by Langesunds Mekaniske Verksted A/S, Langesund, Norway, and was bought by the Monark Line in 1962.

The vertical stem and tall upright funnel marked out the *Monarda* as the oldest of the company's ships. She had been completed as the *Hera* by Oresundsvarvet A/B, Landskrona in 1935. I photographed her at Blaikies Quay in January 1971 after she had arrived from Oulu, Finland, with general cargo, on what was probably one of her last visits to Aberdeen as she was sold to Stena A/B, Gothenburg in April that year.

The *Monark* and *Monita* had both been built in German yards for German owners in 1950. The *Monark* had been completed as the *Possehl* for the Lubeck Linie by Lubecker Flenderwerke, Lubeck and was bought by the Monark Line in 1965 after she had been renamed *Castorp*. The *Monita* had been built by Bremer Vulkan and was originally Richard Adler & Co.'s *Argo* and was acquired by the Monark Line in 1964.

The *Montrose*, which had quadruple expansion steam engines, had been built by N.V. Scheepswerf & Machinefabriek 'De Merwede' Van Vliet & Co. at Hardinxveld, Netherlands as the *Ariel* for Finska Angfartygs A/B of Helsinki. She had an ice-strengthened hull and had been acquired by de Champs in 1968. She was a regular visitor to Aberdeen and also called at other Scottish east coast ports including Grangemouth, Methil and

222

The *Monodora* of 1938 was a regular visitor to Aberdeen on the Monark Line's cargo liner service from the Baltic. She is shown in the Firth of Forth during 1963. *[Don Rowell/Peter Myers collection]*

The Monark Line's *Monarda* of 1935 at Blaikies Quay, Aberdeen, on 11th January 1971 after arriving from Oulu, Finland (left). *[Peter Myers]* The *Monark* of 1950 at Regent Quay, Aberdeen during her first visit to the port in November 1965 (right). Before she was bought by the Monark Line she had been on charter to the Hansa Line for its feeder service between the Persian Gulf and India. *[Aberdeen Journals Ltd.]*

even her namesake port of Montrose. I recall the evocative sight she made as she sailed for Copenhagen from Aberdeen one afternoon in August 1973. She was in ballast and her Maierform bow was clearly exposed.

The *Montrose*, commanded by Captain Jan Linden, made her last call at Aberdeen in January 1974 before she was sold the following month to the London-based Presque Isle Shipping

Co. and was renamed *Kishti Noor* under the Liberian flag. Her departure ended another era at the port as she was the last of the Monark Line's ships to call at Aberdeen.

It wasn't until some years later that I discovered that Aberdeen shipbuilder Hall, Russell and Co. Ltd. had built a Scandinavian-style short sea trader for Norwegian owners in 1953. The *Binna* (1,858g) was completed for

A/S Bonheur (Fred Olsen and Co.), Oslo, and was propelled by a four-cylinder compound steam engine. In appearance she seemed rather dated for a newbuilding of the early 1950s and at first glance could have been easily mistaken for a Hansa A type cargo steamer. In contrast, the cargo steamer *Winga* (2,234/1957) had a more pleasing, modern profile and had been built at the Aberdeen yard of Alexander

Hall and Co. Ltd. for Glen and Co. of Glasgow for their trade from Glasgow and Irish ports to Scandinavian and Baltic countries.

Aberdeen may now be a busier and more prosperous port than when I first became acquainted with it almost 50 years ago, but I still believe that the merchant ships of those days, including the cargo steamers described above, excited my interest in a way that the modern generation of ships can never do.

The Monark Line's *Montrose* of 1954 made her last call at Aberdeen in January 1974. *[Don Rowell/Peter Myers collection]*

STEAM TRAWLERS AT ABERDEEN

In the 1970s I was fortunate to visit Aberdeen several times to photograph the shipping arriving and sailing from the port. There were plenty of smaller motor trawlers still working out of the port but most of the traffic was supply boats - quite a new innovation then.

However, I thought myself lucky in May 1974 to see a few Polish steam trawlers arriving and sailing such as the *Biala* (top). The oil-fired *Biala*, fitted with a compound four-cylinder steam engine, had been completed at Gdansk, Poland, in 1955. By 1979 she had disappeared from the registers.

The bonus of the trip was the British United Trawler *Vanessa* (GY257), completed at Beverley, near Hull, in 1952. Owned by Northern Trawlers Ltd. of Grimsby, she was managed at that time by British United Trawlers Ltd., also of Grimsby. Little did I know she was nearing the end of her days - going to Albert Draper and Sons Ltd. in February of the following year for breaking up.

Behind the foremast of *Vanessa* one can see Aberdeen's Roundhouse, actually octagonal, situated on the North Pier of the harbour entrance. Dating back to 1798 it was built to watch, and get aid if need be, for ships arriving and sailing and continued to do so until 2006 when it was replaced by the new Marine Operations Centre. The tower was almost 'as built' having had only an extra deck and radar added over the years. C-listed, the Harbour Board had plans to demolish the tower but the building was saved by public pressure. Since then the building has been refurbished and is now used by Seacroft Marine Consultants on a long-term tenancy agreement. The old signal lights and radar scanner remain and the beautiful hand-wound clock on the landward side still works.

John Clarkson

BOSUN'S LOCKER

55/01

This sunken, funnel-less steamer proved no problem to identify, and a significant number of our readers have responded, allowing us to tell the full story of her loss. Indeed, one reader phoned with details almost as soon as he received 'Record' 55.

She was indeed sunk at Dar-es-Salaam during the First World War, and turns out to be the twin-screw, passenger-cargo ship *König* (4,820/1896) of Deutsche Ost-Afrika Linie, Hamburg. Completed by Reiherstiegwerft, Hamburg in October 1896, she began work on her owner's Hamburg to Cape Town and Durban service, being used on Durban to Bombay sailings after 1911. On the outbreak of war in August 1914 she was trapped at Dar-es-Salaam by the Royal Navy. One account has her trying to escape on 5th August 1914, but being shelled by the cruiser HMS *Astraea*. Further damage was inflicted by the cruiser HMS *Chatham* on 21st October 1914. On 31st July 1915 her crew tried to scuttle her with explosives in order to block the entrance to Dar-es-Salaam. However, the attempt was a failure as the strong current swung her on to the shore, still leaving a passage into the harbour. Her sinking is generally attributed to shells from the cruiser HMS *Hyacinth* on 17th August 1915.

König was raised after the war (both 1919 and 1921 dates are quoted), and sold for £500 in September 1924 to an Indian company who intended to repair her. However, nothing was done until 1955 when Italian interests took over and broke her up. Photograph 55/01 is believed to have been taken during the First World War.

Thanks to Michael Conway, James Cooper, Brian Hollman, Christy McHale, Alan Savory, Bill Schell, Tony Smythe and Florent von Otterdyk for their responses. Also referred to have been 'East African Wrecks of the First World War' by W.H. Mitchell in 'Sea Breezes', November 1964 (which is mainly concerned with the Royal Navy's pursuit of the cruiser SMS *Koenigsberg*) and Arnold Kludas's 'Die Schiff der Deutschen Afrika-Linien'.

Further views of *König*. [James Cooper collection (top and lower middle), Newall Dunn collection (upper middle and bottom)]

56/01

Reader Alan Savory asks if anyone can identify this stranded Doxford Turret. The photographer was A.W. Ellis of Sidmouth in Devon, yet Alan can find no record of a Turret being wrecked near Sidmouth. Of course, she could well have been refloated as – despite the cliffs – there is sand beneath her keel. One of the editors tentatively identifies the location as just west of Sidmouth, where an old path atop the steep cliffs would provide such a viewpoint. The name appears to have two words of seven and four letters, with the second one beginning *Ha--*, indicating she is one of the Turrets delivered to Edward Nicholl's Cardiff Hall Line. She does not have Nicholl's distinctive markings, and her funnel appears to be plain black, suggesting she is one of those he sold during the First World War (see David Burrell's article on the company in 'British Shipping Fleets'). Just three of these survived the war, *Whateley Hall* (3,712/1904), *Eaton Hall* (3,711/1904) and the second *Grindon*

Hall (3,712/1908), and given the seven letters of the first name, *Grindon Hall* is a distinct possibility. She generally matches the rather poor photograph of this ship on page 156 of 'British Shipping Fleets', but then Turrets were very standardised. From 1915 until her

sale to Greece and renaming in 1920 her owner was the Leadenhall Steam Ship Co. Ltd., managed by McAllum, Soulidi and Co. of London. Can any reader confirm or correct this, admittedly tentative, identification?

56/02

Dated November 1908, the name of the ship in this photograph is quoted as 'Menpai'. A search of the Starke/Schell registers found nothing to match. A close look at the bow appears to confirm her name having six letters. She appears to have steam up but, although not under way or alongside a quay, does not appear to be moving. Beyond her stern is the after-end of another ship, which apparently has no funnel, and in the background there is a crane. Is this the *Memphis*, ex-*America*, of 1891 shortly after arriving at Bo'ness, on the Firth of Forth in November 1908 for scrapping?

These photographs of *Charlesville* of 1951 mentioned in Andrew Bell's article on CMB's 'Congo Boats' in 'Record' 55 show her left at Ango Ango, a small port near to Matadi in West Africa, and right at Teneriffe, Canary Islands, in 1962. *[Jean-Pierre Hack]*

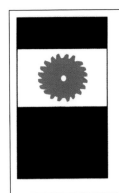 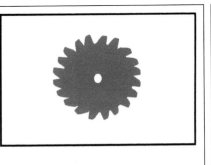  

We don't have many colour pages in this issue but it seemed a pity to miss out on the above flag and funnel colours relating to items in the text. Above left we have the Circular Saw flag and funnel about which Ian Farquhar writes on pages 258, 259 and 260. Above right are the flag and funnel colours for the Great Yarmouth Shipping Co.Ltd. featured on pages 194 to 203. *[Both: J.L. Loughran]*

Other than their most recent ships little was available in colour of ships owned by the Hopemount Shipping Co. Ltd. which featured in 'Record' 54 and 55.

Malcolm Cranfield has kindly sent us the above photograph of *Hoperange* of 1939 sailing from Blyth. Given her pristine appearance, quite possibly the photograph was taken after completion of repairs following the fire and grounding damage she suffered in April 1957.

This letter and accompanying photo have been held over for some time awaiting space in colour pages.

Dunedin model
Regarding the letter from J.D.R. Carruthers in 'Record' 53 about the ship *Dunedin*, attached is a scan of the model of her in the Meat New Zealand head office in Wellington.
IAN J. FARQUHAR, PO Box 92, Dunedin, New Zealand

BRITISH PHOSPHATE CHARTERS

Not unexpectedly, Andrew Bell's article on British Phosphate Commission (BPC) and its ships in 'Record' 53 has attracted much favourable comment, with much on the chartered ships.

Ship details

Nauru Chief was ordered by Thor Thoresen junior, Oslo, and bought by BPC in 1922. She was sunk on 7th June 1942.
Triona (1) was actually sunk by a torpedo.
Triona (2) was torpedoed on 11th January 1944, 300 miles south of Ceylon, but did not sink and reached Fremantle.
Triadic (2) when converted as *Levuka* carried 60 passengers, but in BPC service her capacity was reduced to 41.
IAN J. FARQUHAR, PO Box 92, Dunedin, New Zealand

Bank Line blunder

I found the article on BPC interesting as part of my job was supporting the operation of a phosphoric acid plant, jointly owned by Albright and Wilson and ICI, at Yaraville, Melbourne. The acid was used for fertilizers and industrial phosphates. We used about 120,000 tons of rock each year and had to keep a big stockpile because of the unreliability of regular supplies. Bank Line were frequent carriers but not very popular when the *Northbank* demolished the quay.
TONY SMITH, 24 Balmoral Road, Kingsdown, near Deal, Kent CT14 8DB

Comparisons

I really enjoyed the article on the BPC ships and have always been fascinated by the company and its ships. I always thought the Harland and Wolf ships were unusual but fine looking. I had never thought that they compared in looks to Port Line ships, but they do. Talking of comparisons I thought the Nauru Shipping Company's *Eigamoiya* looked very like Ellerman's last *City of London* and *City of Hull*. Very sad to learn how the islanders squandered their income from the BPC.
BOB HUGHES by e-mail.

Post 1968 charters

During my time at sea I spent a good length of time on ships hauling phosphate from Nauru and Christmas Island to Australia and New Zealand. I therefore found the article by Andrew Bell on BPC in 'Record' 53 very interesting. The photographs as usual are excellent.

To say that BPC's last involvement in shipping was in 1968 with the chartering of the *Valetta* is, I think, incorrect. Partners in Scottish Ship Management (SSM), Lyle Shipping Co. and H. Hogarth and Sons, were both associated with BPC for a number of years and this was continued after SSM was formed in 1968. Other British and Scandinavian companies also had longstanding dealings with BPC. As far as SSM was concerned, contracts of affreightment were the usual form of agreement.

In 1971 the newly-built Lambert Brothers' bulk carrier *Temple Hall*, then managed by SSM, was placed on a five-year bareboat charter to BPC with Australian seafarers employed on the ship. In 1974, after the management agreement with SSM was terminated by Lambert Brothers, the ship came off hire. She was replaced in 1974 by the *Cape Hawke* which, whilst being re-engined in Amsterdam, had extra accommodation built on to bring her up to Australian manning requirements. The *Cape Hawke* remained on charter with BPC until 1981 when the charter finished and the ship was bareboat chartered to Australian National Line (ANL). This continued until December 1986 when the charter finished and the ship was broken up in Kaohsiung.

The *Baron Pentland* of 1976 was one of four sister ships built in Govan for Lyle and Hogarth. She was slightly different from the other three in that the accommodation block was larger to meet Australian requirements. She was placed on bareboat charter with BPC, again with Australian seafarers. She remained on charter for about a year until two newbuilds in Japan were delivered and placed on ten-year bareboat charters with BPC. These were the *Cape Otway* in 1976 and *Baron Murray* in 1977, built with specific design features to satisfy BPC.

Chartered to BPC as a replacement for *Triaster, Temple Hall* wears Scottish Ship Management's funnel colours. Completed by Upper Clyde Shipbuilders in June 1971, she had an interesting life, with her original Ruston and Hornsby engines being replaced with Stork-Werkspoor diesels after just three years. In 1978 she was converted in Norway to a pipe burying vessel, *Seaway Sandpiper*, a name shortened to *Sandpiper* in 1990. This extended her life considerably, and as this edition was being finalised in September 2013, she was being delivered to Aliaga for demolition. *[Kingsley Barr/Russell Priest]*

The *Cape Otway* and *Baron Murray* remained on charter to BPC until 1981 when they along with the *Cape Hawke* had their charters terminated and were taken on bareboat charter by ANL. It appeared that the three ships continued transporting phosphate although other cargoes may have been carried. The two survived with ANL until 1987 when both were sold for further trading.

As stated in the article, it was in 1981 that the *Valetta* finished her charter with BPC, the same year that the three SSM ships were transferred to ANL charters. BPC's last involvement with shipping did not take place in 1968 with the chartering of the *Valetta* but in 1977 with the chartering of the *Baron Murray*.

After a succession of owners and names, the *Cape Otway* was broken up as the *Pearl of Ajman* at Alang in 2003 and the *Baron Murray*, as *Glory Falcon*, was broken up in Chittagong, Bangladesh during 2009.

Whilst on charter to BPC all ships carried the SSM funnel markings although the *Temple Hall* may have carried Lambert's funnel at the start of the charter. The three ships which went on charter to ANL carried the ANL funnel.

The photograph of *Cape Hawke* on page 48 shows her in the early funnel colours of SSM and before the extra accommodation was built on.

JOHN DRURY, 6 Grenville Way, Whitley Bay, Tyne and Wear NE26 3JJ

Seen at Fremantle, the Haugesund-built *Cape Hawke* replaced BPC's *Tri-Ellis*. Delivered in 1971, she had a short life, broken up at Kaohsiung in 1986 still as *Cape Hawke*. *[Ted Drake/Russell Priest]*

Photographed at Hobart, *Baron Pentland* was on charter to BPC in 1976 and 1977 in succession to *Temple Hall*. The Cardiff-class bulker was delivered to Hogarth by Govan Shipbuilders Ltd. in June 1976, and fitted with a Harland and Wolff diesel. Sale in 1983 saw her become the Greek *Evangelos L*, subsequently moving to China as *Hua Zhen*. By 2012 she was listed as 'continued existence in doubt'. *[Kingsley Barr/Russell Priest]*

Photographed at Hobart, the Mitsui-built *Cape Otway* of 1976 was chartered as a replacement for BPC's *Triadic*. *[Kingsley Barr/ Russell Priest]*

Baron Murray, sister of *Cape Otway*, was delivered in April 1977 and replaced *Baron Pentland* on BPC charter. *[Kingsley Barr/ Russell Priest]*

Earlier generations of Hogarth's 'Barons' also carried phosphate for BPC, and the photographs on this page were both taken in Australian waters. The steamer *Baron Belhaven* was the second of the name, completed in 1924 by Lithgows Ltd. when Hogarth's had a burst of post-war optimism and expanded their fleet massively. Unlike many other owners, they never laid up any of their ships during the Depression. *Baron Belhaven* remained with Hogarths until 1957, when sold to become *Pacific Skipper*. She was broken up in Japan during 1963. *[Jim Freeman]*

Third of the name, *Baron Jedburgh* was delivered by John Readhead and Sons Ltd. in October 1956. She was the seventh of fourteen completed to this attractive design, and the first motor ship of the series, distinguished by a smaller, 'streamlined' funnel. Sold in 1967, N. Tsimplis first named her *Evie G. Chimples*, and later *Global Mariner*. After stranding whilst on a voyage from Nantes to Assab with wheat on 30th December 1978, she was towed into Massawa where she was eventually broken up. *[John Mathieson/Russell Priest]*

Later to become partners with Hogarths in Scottish Ship Management, Lyle Shipping Co. Ltd. also had a history of working for BPC, who from the 1950s was Lyle's most important customer. *Cape Grenville* (top) was delivered in 1949 by Lithgows Ltd., who were initially joint owners. She was sold in 1965 to become *Cosmar* and a string of names followed: *Cosmaria*, *Selas*, *Naya* and *Mayfair* until she was broken up at Gadani Beach in 1980. *[David Kirby]*

Cape Horn was photographed on 2nd December 1965, with hatches open ready for discharge (middle). The 1957 motor ship was another Lithgows completion, albeit with redesigned superstructure. Sold to Stathatos and Co. in 1967 as *South Venture*, on 22nd October 1972 she stranded on Roncador Cay, off the east coast of Nicaragua, and was declared a constructive total loss. *[David Kirby]*

Cape Hawke was from an earlier generation of Lithgow motor ships, completed at Port Glasgow in March 1941 and was again partly financed by the builder (bottom). Sold in 1963, her 22 years under Lyle management was impressive for a war-built ship. After sale to N.A. Valmas, first as *Kalliopi* and then as *Roy*, she might have carried on longer, but fractured her crankshaft in 1967 and was subsequently sold for breaking up in Japan *[Lindsay Rex]*

Cape Clear, seen at Geelong (above), was unusual for Lyle in being a second-hand purchase. She was completed as *Derryclare* at Burntisland in 1946, having the distinctive 'beaked' bow favoured by owners McCowen and Gross Ltd. In Lyle's fleet from 1952 to 1962, the Doxford-powered *Cape Clear* was then sold to Hong Kong owners as *Golden Sigma*, later becoming *Laurel*. She was demolished at Hong Kong in 1967. *[William Volum/Russell Priest]*

Lyle was allowed to continue ordering from Lithgows during wartime, but comparison of the 1943-built *Cape Howe* below with *Cape Hawke* opposite reveals a certain austerity about the *Cape Howe's* bridge. She was a steamer, and became the last of this type in Lyle's fleet when sold in July 1961 to Hong Kong owners who renamed her *World Pink*. She was broken up at Kaohsiung in 1967. *[Lindsay Rex/Russell Priest]*

Andrew Weir's Bank Line also found BPC a good customer, and there are accounts of their ships leaving the UK and making so many trips between Ocean Island and Australia that, when they returned to the UK, first trip apprentices had finished their time and were now fourth mates. Seen underway to Risdon on 1st May 1959, *Edenbank* was one of no fewer than 12 Liberties in the fleet, making Bank Line the largest British commercial operator of the type. Completed in December 1943 as *Samtroy* for the Ministry of War Transport, Bank bought her in 1947 and sold her to China in 1960. Under her final name, *Zhan Dou 43*, she survived until broken up in 1987, leading to speculation that she was the very last Liberty to trade commercially. *[Lindsay Rex/Russell Priest].*

Roybank was a Doxford motorship, more or less contemporary with *Edenbank*, delivered to Bank Line just a year after the Liberty was completed. She had a similar layout to the US-built ship, with a composite superstructure and three hatches ahead of the bridge. Her design was similar to Doxford's successful 'Economy' type, but had the forecastle lacking on this type. She was photographed discharging at Risdon on 18th June 1960. *Roybank* was sold to C.S. Koo, Hong Kong, in 1962 as *Silver Lake*, and was broken up at Kaohsiung in 1968. *[Lindsay Rex/Russell Priest].*

Moraybank of 1945 was also a wartime product of Doxfords, but from her rather anachronistic split superstructure she appears to be one of the 'Improved Economy' type, still with the three-cylinder oil engine fitted to the earlier 'Economy' type and to *Roybank*. Sold to Taiwan owners in 1963 to become *Hsing Yung*, she was scrapped at Kaohsiung five years later. She was underway from Risdon on 30th April 1960 when photographed. *[Lindsay Rex]*

Photographed at Hobart on 10th September 1962, *Southbank* of 1948 was the second new motorship delivered to Bank Line after the Second World War, again a Doxford product. She was unfortunate enough to be stranded on Washington Island in the Pacific on Boxing Day 1964 whilst on a voyage from Port Pirie to the United Kingdom with general cargo. She broke in two on New Year's Eve. *[David Kirby]*

TALBOT-BOOTH
Roy Fenton

To have books familiarly referred to by your name must be the ultimate accolade for an author, and amongst maritime books 'Talbot-Booth' shares this distinction with 'Lloyd's', 'Jane's' and possibly 'Mitchell and Sawyer'. This article offers a provisional account of E.C. Talbot-Booth's prolific output of merchant ship identification books, and considers their usefulness. It is provisional simply because there may well be more to know about the author and his work. The early story of the books is complex, and it is possible that editions may be more numerous than are listed here – the writer has not been able to find or examine every title or edition from the late 1930s. 'Record' would be delighted to hear from those who know more.

Like any long running series of books, 'Talbot-Booths' evolved over time. Titles changed, major features came and went, whilst coverage expanded – sometimes significantly. Changes of publishers probably contributed to this, although in their final incarnations the books stayed remarkably consistent in style.

The listing of books below is in order of original title, roughly in the sequence in which each was first published, and is chronological within each title. When a date alongside the title is shown in bold it appears as part of the book's title. Dates not in bold are from publication dates quoted within the book, and those in brackets are estimates.

Ships of the British Merchant Navy: Passenger Liners 1932

This is the first known book by Talbot-Booth, who was assisted by E.B.R. Sargeant. Its 592 pages (9 by 6 inches) have 64 colour plates and 234 scale drawings to a scale of 150 feet to 1 inch.

The book sets out to be a guide to recognition of individual ships. Companies are grouped by colour of funnels, with black coming first. For each company there is a brief history, lists of their current fleet (passenger and cargo), and detailed descriptions of their livery, down to such features as ventilators. There is a colour profile of a ship from each company, followed by black and white drawings of each class. The definition of a 'passenger ship' is quite liberal, with many cargo liners represented which carried the standard 12 passengers, and even some Blue Funnel ships which catered for only four.

The publisher was Andrew Melrose, London, who produced a very tidy book. Talbot-Booth's introduction – typical of later volumes which speak of plans not always realised – notes that it is intended to devote further volumes to cargo ships, cross-channel and short-sea vessels and principal foreign fleets. It was to be four years before such coverage was achieved, and it was not with this publisher. The published price is not known, but as five shillings from the sale of each was to be donated to the Royal National Lifeboat Institute, it could not have been cheap in 1932.

British Merchant Ships 1934

Two years later, Talbot-Booth's publisher and concept changed. The 220 landscape pages of 'British Merchant Ships' begin with four colour pages featuring 226 drawings of funnels and flags. Almost half the book is taken up with 667 drawings of ships to a scale of 150 feet to one inch, beginning with seven pages of coloured drawings (see opposite). The drawings are grouped initially by the ship's funnel colours and then by other features. To call the drawings slightly naïve is not to disparage them, as they are accurate and detailed although a little foreshortened, and sheer is often omitted. Beneath each drawing are listed the names of the ship or ships depicted, tonnages, dimensions, details of machinery, builders and owners.

Eighty pages are devoted to an alphabetical list of British and Dominion ship owners, listing their addresses, current fleets, their services, details of colour schemes and, for many, a brief history. Most deep-sea liner and tramp companies are included, as are major coastal and short-sea liner operators, but not coastal tramps. There is a glossary and an index of ships.

The publisher was Rich and Cowan, London and particularly noticeable are the advertisements before and after the text, 86 pages of them offering a remarkable range of goods and services to shipping companies and seafarers, from bunker suppliers to bookmakers.

It is possible that a second edition of 'British Merchant Ships' appeared in 1937, but a bookseller's catalogue which lists it may well have confused it with the second edition of its successor 'Merchant Ships'.

The British Merchant Navy (circa 1935)

This appears to be a reduced edition of 'British Merchant Ships', with no advertisements and no introduction, and by a new publisher, Sampson Low, Marston and Co. Ltd. It begins with 279 illustrations of funnel colours and house flags, very similar in format to the 1934 'British Merchant Ships', but with some omissions. Clearly, most of the original drawings were re-used. It continues with a total of 707 coloured and black and white drawings of ships, most but not all of those used in 'British Merchant Ships 1934', although the pages are laid out differently. There are no company listings and no index. There is no date on the writer's edition, but a bookseller's catalogue dates it, probably correctly, to about 1935.

The British Merchant Navy 1937-8

In this expanded edition the number of flag and funnel illustrations has grown to 426. The original artwork for these was reused, with some drawings simply dropped, and a large number of others added at the end, spoiling the colour sequence. There are now 880 drawings of ships, fully indexed.

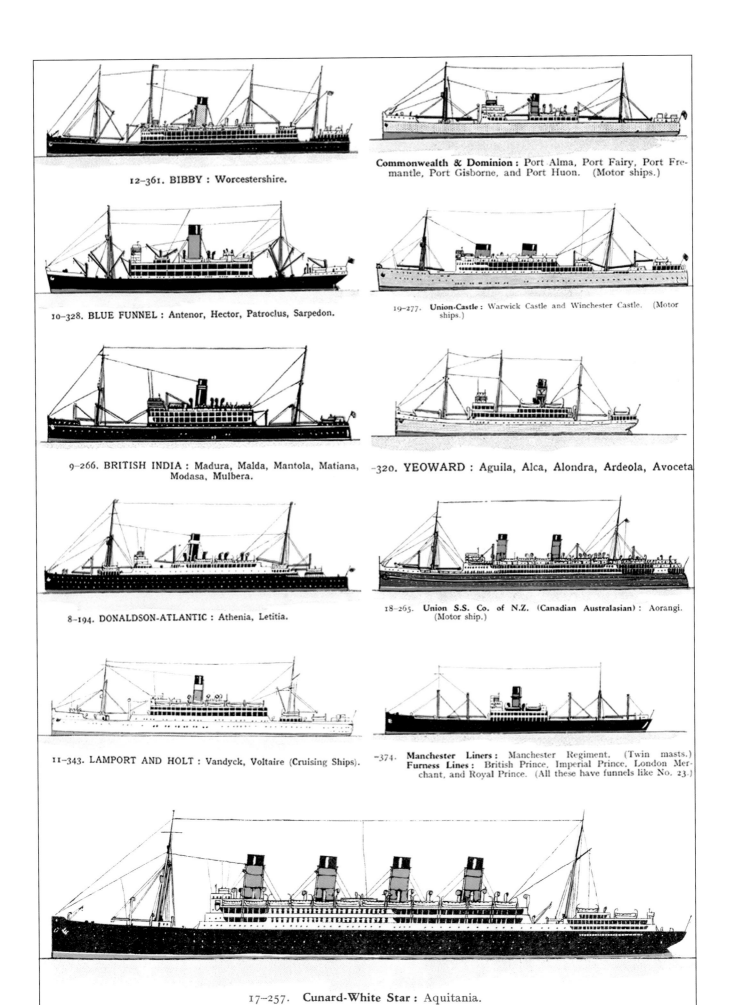

12-361. BIBBY : Worcestershire.

Commonwealth & Dominion : Port Alma, Port Fairy, Port Fremantle, Port Gisborne, and Port Huon. (Motor ships.)

10-328. BLUE FUNNEL : Antenor, Hector, Patroclus, Sarpedon.

19-277. **Union-Castle :** Warwick Castle and Winchester Castle. (Motor ships.)

9-266. BRITISH INDIA : Madura, Malda, Mantola, Matiana, Modasa, Mulbera.

-320. YEOWARD : Aguila, Alca, Alondra, Ardeola, Avoceta

8-194. DONALDSON-ATLANTIC : Athenia, Letitia.

18-265. Union S.S. Co. of N.Z. (Canadian Australasian) : Aorangi. (Motor ship.)

11-343. LAMPORT AND HOLT : Vandyck, Voltaire (Cruising Ships).

-374. **Manchester Liners :** Manchester Regiment. (Twin masts.) **Furness Lines :** British Prince, Imperial Prince, London Merchant, and Royal Prince. (All these have funnels like No. 23.)

17-257. **Cunard-White Star :** Aquitania.

Samples of the coloured drawings from 'British Merchant Ships 1934' and the 1937 edition of 'The British Merchant Navy'.
These scans have not been reproduced to scale.

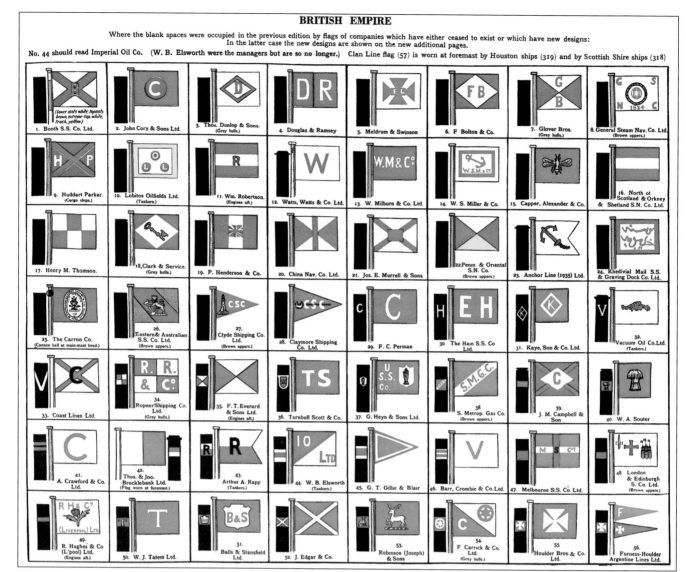

Coloured illustrations of house flags and funnels were a feature of Talbot-Booth books in the 1930s. Those above were scanned from 'British Merchant Ships 1934', and also appear in editions of 'House-flags and Funnels of British and Foreign Shipping Companies' from 1935 to 1937.

House-flags and Funnels of British and Foreign Shipping Companies (1935 to 1937)

This series re-uses the flag and funnel illustrations from the contemporary editions of 'The British Merchant Navy', adding to them many more from around the world. There are also representative coloured drawings of ships from the major maritime nations, mostly large passenger ships, including the British ones from 'The British Merchant Navy'. Sampson Low, Marston and Co. Ltd. were again the publishers. Only the 1937 edition is dated, but booksellers' and library catalogues indicate there were also editions in 1935 and, possibly, 1936.

Merchant Ships 1936

For this new title, the format of 'British Merchant Ships' was vastly expanded to offer coverage of the ships and companies of many other nations. The title page boasts of '690 colour illustrations and 1,268 line drawings by the editor'. Although, when sister ships are accounted for, many more than 1,268 ships are covered, it appears that coverage of non-British fleets is selective; Denmark, for instance, is represented by just 34 drawings. Nevertheless, this is a substantial and weighty volume, and was a milestone in the evolution of 'Talbot-Booths' in including ships from around the world (although by no means all of them). Although still foreshortened, many drawings show more maturity, and the better ones are delightful.

Merchant Ships 1937

According to a bookseller's listing, this enlarged edition has 942 coloured illustrations and 1,560 'silhouettes'.

Merchant Ships 1939

The coloured drawings of funnels and house flags are omitted (in fact, they may have disappeared in 1937), replaced by black and white, colour-coded drawings of funnels. This feature is imported from another Talbot-Booth production, 'Ships and the Sea' (described below).

Merchant Ships 1940

The introduction notes that it was intended to completely re-organise this edition, so that ships are grouped by number and by colour of funnels, regardless of nationality. This scheme was abandoned on the outbreak of war, the introduction continues, not because ships were now routinely painted grey, but because neutral ships had their national colours and names painted so prominently that there was no doubt about their identity. However, within each national grouping the drawings are still organised by the ships' funnel colours. Clearly, this 1940 publication was rapidly overtaken by events.

Over 800 new ship drawings and 50 photographs are added, again according to the introduction, but none of

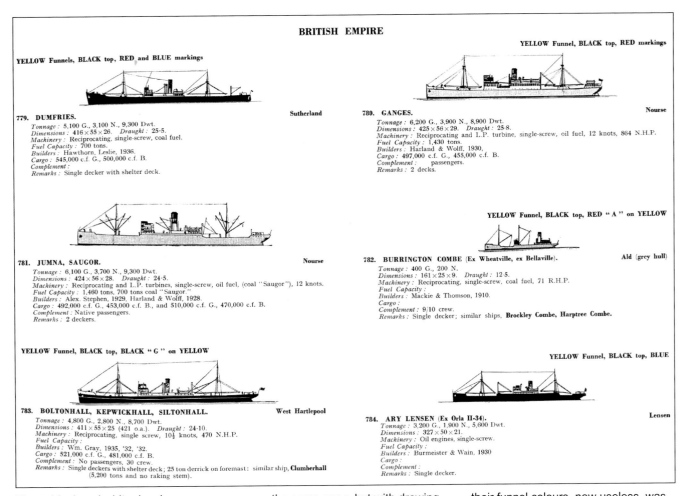

YELLOW Funnels, BLACK top, RED and BLUE markings

779. DUMFRIES.   Sutherland
Tonnage : 5,100 G., 3,100 N., 9,300 Dwt.
Dimensions : 416 × 55 × 26.   *Draught :* 25·5.
Machinery : Reciprocating, single-screw, coal fuel.
Fuel Capacity : 700 tons.
Builders : Hawthorn, Leslie, 1936.
Cargo : 545,000 c.f. G., 500,000 c.f. B.
Complement :
Remarks : Single decker with shelter deck.

781. JUMNA, SAUGOR.   Nourse
Tonnage : 6,100 G., 3,700 N., 9,300 Dwt.
Dimensions : 424 × 56 × 28.   *Draught :* 24·5.
Machinery : Reciprocating and L.P. turbines, single-screw, oil fuel, (coal "Saugor"), 12 knots.
Fuel Capacity : 1,460 tons, 700 tons coal "Saugor."
Builders : Alex. Stephen, 1929, Harland & Wolff, 1928.
Cargo : 492,000 c.f. G., 453,000 c.f. B., and 510,000 c.f. G., 470,000 c.f. B.
Complement : Native passengers.
Remarks : 2 deckers.

YELLOW Funnel, BLACK top, BLACK "G" on YELLOW

783. BOLTONHALL, KEPWICKHALL, SILTONHALL.   West Hartlepool
Tonnage : 4,800 G., 2,800 N., 8,700 Dwt.
Dimensions : 411 × 55 × 25 (421 o.a.).   *Draught :* 24·10.
Machinery : Reciprocating, single screw, 10½ knots, 470 N.H.P.
Fuel Capacity :
Builders : Wm. Gray, 1935, '32, '32.
Cargo : 521,000 c.f. G., 481,000 c.f. B.
Complement : No passengers, 30 crew.
Remarks : Single deckers with shelter deck ; 25 ton derrick on foremast ; similar ship, **Clumberhall** (5,200 tons and no raking stem).

YELLOW Funnel, BLACK top, RED markings

780. GANGES.   Nourse
Tonnage : 6,200 G., 3,900 N., 8,900 Dwt.
Dimensions : 425 × 56 × 29.   *Draught :* 25·8.
Machinery : Reciprocating and L.P. turbine, single-screw, oil fuel, 12 knots, 864 N.H.P.
Fuel Capacity : 1,430 tons.
Builders : Harland & Wolff, 1930,
Cargo : 497,000 c.f. G., 455,000 c.f. B.
Complement :   passengers.
Remarks : 2 decks.

YELLOW Funnel, BLACK top, RED "A" on YELLOW

782. BURRINGTON COMBE (Ex Wheatville, ex Bellaville).   Ald (grey hull)
Tonnage : 400 G., 200 N.
Dimensions : 161 × 25 × 9.   *Draught :* 12·5.
Machinery : Reciprocating, single-screw, coal fuel, 71 R.H.P.
Fuel Capacity :
Builders : Mackie & Thomson, 1910.
Cargo :
Complement : 9/10 crew.
Remarks : Single decker ; similar ships, **Brockley Combe, Harptree Combe.**

YELLOW Funnel, BLACK top, BLUE

784. ARY LENSEN (Ex Orla II-34).   Lensen
Tonnage : 3,200 G., 1,900 N., 5,600 Dwt.
Dimensions : 327 × 50 × 21.
Machinery : Oil engines, single-screw.
Fuel Capacity :
Builders : Burmeister & Wain, 1930
Cargo :
Complement :
Remarks : Single decker.

These black and white drawings are from the 'The British Merchant Navy 1937-8', but were re-used repeatedly. For instance, 'Merchant Ships 1940' uses the same ones, but with drawing 782 of *Burrington Combe* omitted. This was odd, because she was not a war loss. The classification of ships by their funnel colours, now useless, was dropped following the 1940 edition.

the new drawings are of British Empire ships 'at the request of the authorities'. Over 300 new black and white funnel drawings are added, making a total of 1,124, and these exactly match those in the seventh edition of 'Ships and the Sea' (described below).

One of the foibles of the author, which make the books even more interesting, is his penchant for adding slightly quirky lists, and in this edition these include names of tug, salvage and whaling companies, British trawler owners, and European fishing vessel port distinguishing letters. There is a surprisingly complete chronological list of British war losses up to April 1940, plus silhouettes of German aircraft.

The author was assisted in this and other wartime editions by E.B.R. Sargeant, almost certainly a former colleague from the Royal Navy.

An edition of 'Merchant Ships' published 'in the early summer of 1941' is mentioned in the introduction to the 1942 edition, but has not been found in libraries or in booksellers' catalogues, and the date was probably a mistake on the part of the author, who had much work to do for the 1942 edition.

Merchant Ships 1942

This edition represented another milestone, in that the 2,208 ship drawings were completely re-arranged. Regardless of nationality, these are ordered according to a rather complex system based on funnels, masts, hull structure, position of engines and other features, a system which is explained only briefly in the foreword. This was the precursor of the revised 'Talbot-Booth' coding system that emerged in post-war years.

Although 'many additional half-tones have been introduced', according to the foreword, 'it has not been permitted to include a list of war losses and no new drawings of ships have been allowed'. However, the long section listing companies and their ships (still grouped by nationality) is enhanced with additional entries and many more black and white drawings of house flags plus photographs of ships in pre-war colours. In the British Empire section, a few foreign ships are listed under the British owners who managed them on behalf of the Ministry of War Transport, but only four 'Empire' ships are listed, and none are drawn.

The rate at which new editions were appearing seems to have outpaced the editor's ability to keep track of the changes, as there is no sign of any of the 'very large number of funnel designs' which were added, according to the foreword and the list of contents. Details of funnel colours are another feature rendered superfluous by wartime events. In the US, this and the two subsequent editions were published by Macmillan in New York.

Merchant Ships 1943

The artwork for most pages is identical to that for 1942, and the number of drawings is virtually unchanged, but a few minor changes can be found here and there.

Merchant Ships 1944

In the last of the wartime editions few if any changes have been made from the 1943 edition, although a new editorial was written. This admits that once again the editor cannot make changes because a list of war losses had not been published. Very few war-built ships are added, and for instance just seven 'Empires' are included.

Merchant Ships 1949-50

The first post-war edition, again from Sampson Low, Marston and Co. Ltd., is notable for a format change from landscape to portrait, although the pages are almost square, actually 11¾ inches deep and 10 inches wide. There appear to be fewer drawings than in the wartime editions, possibly because much of the author's collection was destroyed during the war when his publisher's offices were bombed, and photos still feature extensively in this edition. Much space is devoted to brief accounts of major companies, sometimes with histories and routes, but always with black and white drawings of flags and funnels plus other livery details. The editorial is proud of the fact that the price has been halved compared with the 1944 edition, presumably because the target audience was now enthusiasts rather than the military, allowing an extended print run.

Presumably as a result of wartime experience, the identification system has been developed to rely largely on the sequence of masts, kingpost and funnel. Thus, a 'Liberty', with just a stump foremast but topmasts on the other two masts, is coded KMFM; one with three topmasts MMFM. The ships are grouped in alphabetical order of such codings, so that KKFM precedes KMFM. Within these groupings, ships are sequenced according to their hull form, with the flush-decked 'Liberty' being coded simply H, and a ship with only a forecastle being H1. This system was perpetuated and developed, becoming the definitive 'Talbot-Booth system'.

A war loss list is included, confined to ships over 500 tons and with German and Japanese losses specifically excluded. An odd feature in a book dedicated to ship recognition is a list, by builder, of ships under construction. This seems to have been an attempt to bring the book up to date as many of the ships listed have received names and a fair number are noted as being completed in 1948, whereas the identification drawings are noted as being updated to May 1949. A US edition was published by McGraw-Hill.

Merchant Ships 1959

The first edition published by the Journal of Commerce and Shipping Telegraph reverts to a landscape format and has

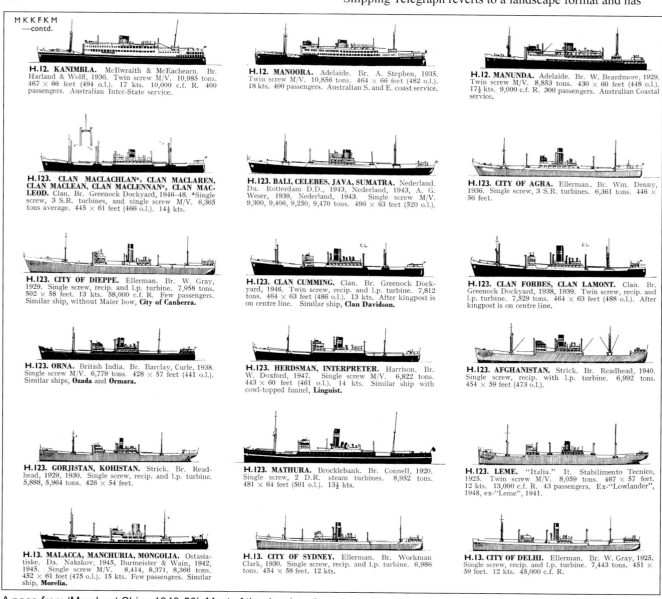

A page from 'Merchant Ships 1949-50'. Most of the drawings have been newly executed, the originals of prewar ships being destroyed in an air raid. Relevant ones from this edition were reused in the 1959 and 1963 editions.

INDEX TO RECORD 53 TO 56

Issue numbers are shown in bold

Index of ships

All ships' names in the text are listed, including proposed or other names not actually used, which are shown in brackets. Wherever possible, dates of build or other information are given to identify merchant ships. Ships listed in photo offers are not indexed.

Dromore Castle - see page 255. *[Amgueddfa Cymru-National Museum Wales DI011159]*